George Gordon Byron

The corsair

George Gordon Byron

The corsair

ISBN/EAN: 9783337821890

Printed in Europe, USA, Canada, Australia, Japan

Cover: Foto ©ninafisch / pixelio.de

More available books at **www.hansebooks.com**

"World Classics"

The Corsair
Lara

LORD BYRON

Illustrations by Gambard and Mittis

With Introduction by M. F. Sweetser

BOSTON
JOSEPH KNIGHT COMPANY
M DCCC XCIII

Contents.

THE CORSAIR.

	Page
INTRODUCTION	xi
CANTO THE FIRST	1
CANTO THE SECOND	28
CANTO THE THIRD	54

LARA.

CANTO THE FIRST	87
CANTO THE SECOND	116

INTRODUCTION.

UPON the altars of unseemly and deformed human souls sometimes flashes the divinest white light of genius, and dwells and burns there for years, as if immeasurably superior to, unconscious of, the blemishes about it. Thus it was with Byron. Poisoned by evil heredities on both sides, ill-trained in youth, an associate of atheists, his great soul bore many wounds and scars, and yet was the abode of transcendent genius.

The family history begins with Ralph de Burun, whose name was recorded in Domesday Book, away back in the days of the Norman Conquest. Some of his descendants became knights, and in their posterity the family rose to the rank of baronets. Still later, they did valiant service for the king, in the stormy days of Charles I., and that grateful sovereign raised them to the peerage. Coming down to the eighteenth century, we find the family represented by William Lord Byron and his brother, the celebrated Admiral Byron, the grand-uncle and the grandfather of the poet. The admiral's son was Captain John Byron, of the Guards, who made a runaway match with Lady Caermarthen, and kindly married her, after she had secured a divorce. To them was born a daughter, Augusta Mary, who became the Honourable Mrs. Leigh. The second wife of the dissolute guardsman was Catharine Gordon of Gight, a wealthy Scottish lady, in whose veins ran the blood of the Stuarts. From this union was born the author of "Childe Harold," who first saw the light in Holles Street, London, January 22d, 1788.

It did not take the captain long to squander the fortune of his Highland bride, and then he lightly abandoned her, levanting to the Continent, where he died, at Valenciennes, in 1791. Embittered by her wrongs, and withal by nature of a moody and violent spirit, Catharine returned to Aberdeen with her infant son (whom in angry moments she called "a lame brat"), and at the age of five the unhappy child was put to school. Long before he reached college, he had passed thrice under the domination of the master-passion of his life, in his love-affairs with Mary Duff, Margaret Parker, and Miss Chaworth.

When George had reached the age of ten, his grand-uncle, the reigning Lord Byron, died without a son, and his title descended to the son of Captain Byron. The lad was thence known as Baron Byron of Rochdale, with a large encumbered property, and the lordship of Newstead Abbey, in Nottinghamshire. He became a ward in Chancery, with the Earl of Carlisle as guardian. Mrs. Byron, who made his life miserable by alternate petting and scolding, each equally spasmodic and without reason, kept him at Newstead for a year, studying Latin; and then placed him in Dr. Glennie's school, at Dulwich, near London. But she so often withdrew the young student, to take him to masquerades and other fashionable amusements, that his lessons suffered, and Lord Carlisle therefore caused him to be sent to the more firmly ruled school at Harrow. Here he remained three years, a turbulent and ill-conditioned pupil, and without scholastic aptitude, but generous to his mates, and devoted to miscellaneous reading. Thereafter, he gave two years to a rather idle life at Trinity College, Cambridge, devoting himself more to hearty practice in fencing, boxing, swimming shooting, and kindred diversions than to the study of the classics and the humanities. In 1809 he took his seat in the House of Lords, and had a serious purpose of entering politics, under which impulse he made three rather good speeches before the Peers. But this career was soon closed, for he had already unwittingly entered upon a grander mission, whose swift and resistless advance swept away all other plans and dreams.

The drift of his mind toward poetry showed itself as early as his tenth year, when he gratified his wrath at a certain old lady by writing a rhymed satire. His childish love-affairs also naturally stirred the fountains of verse. In his eighteenth year he printed a little volume of miscellaneous verses, but a kindly old clerical mentor objected to the unchasteness which appeared therein, and the young author caused the edition to be destroyed. In 1807 he published "Hours of Idleness," a volume of very poor verse, which showed but scanty promise for the future. Brougham or some other critic on the "Edinburgh Review" received this poor little book with a harsh and chaffing critique; and Byron answered with the sharp satire entitled "English Bards and Scotch Reviewers," which created a great sensation in British literary circles. In this work, the nettled young poet opened hot batteries of abuse against many famous literary contemporaries, an achievement for which in after years he was heartily sorry.

In the summer of 1809, Byron began his first long tour in Europe, attended by his friend Hobhouse (afterwards Lord Broughton). Landing at Lisbon, they crossed Spain, and travelled onward to Albania and the cities of Greece and Asia Minor, visiting Yannina, Parnassus, Delphi, Athens, Smyrna, and Constantinople. His introduction to Ali Pasha, his life among the Franciscan monks, his swimming from Sestos to Abydos, and the composition of the first two cantos of "Childe Harold," were among the remarkable features of this romantic journey of more than two years' duration. This fragment of "Childe Harold" was published in London in 1812, and

INTRODUCTION.

exactly hit the popular taste. As the author wrote: " I awoke one morning, and found myself famous." Byron was borne aloft on the vast wave of enthusiasm, and became the lion of the drawing-rooms and clubs, a dandy, a lady-killer, and a man of fashion.

In 1813 Byron made an offer of marriage to the daughter of Sir Ralph Milbanke, a Baronet in the County of Durham. She was not only a person of great prospective wealth (since her mother was sister and co-heiress of Lord Wentworth), but had been finely educated, and was a paragon of many virtues. She astonished the aspiring suitor by declining his offer; and yet the two young people continued their correspondence, on the basis of Platonic friendship. After more than a year, during which time Byron had proposed to and been rejected by another woman, he made a second attempt at winning Miss Milbanke, and this time unfortunately succeeded. They were married January 2d, 1815, and lived together but a single year. At first, he admired his patrician bride, and almost loved her; but he soon found his pleasures away from home, where incompatibilities of character developed amain. His

INTRODUCTION.

extravagance resulted in nine executions being placed in his house during this single year. Lady Byron, wounded to the quick by his astonishing conduct, charitably supposed that he was insane, until a careful investigation and enquiries showed that he was perfectly sane, but extraordinarily corrupt. Lady Byron stated to Harriet Beecher Stowe that before his marriage he entered upon an unfortunate intrigue with his half-sister, Mrs. Leigh, and that this amour was kept up openly after the marriage. This ghastly story is not regarded either as proven or as discredited, because there is some evidence for it, and apparently more against it. Mr. Lushington, the lawyer, advised Lady Byron to secure a separation, for some unknown reason. In December she gave birth to a daughter, Augusta Ada, afterwards Countess of Lovelace; and the very next month she went to her father's country estate, from whence she wrote to her husband that she would never live with him again. It is believed that the deserted man bore the loss quite without anguish.

After Lady Byron's separation, a wild storm of social acrimony burst around the poet, until then such a universal favourite. Perhaps the Leigh matter was known and believed by the society leaders, for scarcely anything else can account for the loathing and contempt with which Byron was hooted out of sight. Full of defiant pride, with his heart almost breaking the dethroned favourite left England in April, 1816. It was his desire and his destiny never to return.

Landing at Ostend, the exile ascended the Rhine, in the companionship of his travelling physician, Dr. Polidori. During a sojourn near the Lake of Geneva, he met Shelley and Miss Godwin (Mrs. Shelley). In their company was Miss Clairmont, by whom Byron had a daughter, Allegra.

During this pleasant summer by the lake the poet composed the third canto of " Childe Harold," " The Prisoner of Chillon," and " Manfred."

Another long episode of his life passed at Venice, where he dwelt for most of the next three years, — a period in which he mingled the loftiest and richest poetic work with a career of low and miscellaneous debauchery. During this period he wrote " The Lament of Tasso,"

"Beppo," "Mazeppa," and four cantos of
"Don Juan," which is perhaps the grandest
and most original of his works. This unrivalled masterpiece was issued in instalments,
and anonymously, and received the maledictions and wrathful reproaches of most critics.

While at Venice Byron delivered to Moore a
manuscript autobiography, chiefly concerned
with his married life, and abounding in spicy
details concerning well-known English personages. Moore disposed of this treasure-trove
to John Murray, the publisher, but that gentleman, after consulting with Mrs. Leigh and the
writer's executor, consigned the work to the
flames. Much of it was of such a nature that
it could never have been published.

The grand passion of Byron's life, and that in
which he showed strongest constancy and feeling, was his love for the Countess Guiccioli,
the young and beautiful daughter of Count
Gamba, and the wife of the wealthy old Count
Guiccioli, a noble of the Romagna. She was
a singularly attractive blonde, with abundant
golden hair; a creature of infinite sentiment,
unusual sweetness of character, warmth of
affection, and disinterestedness. Byron and

La Guiccioli met early in the year 1819, and they fell desperately in love with each other. An ardent intrigue immediately sprang up between them, and within little more than a year the Countess secured from the Pope a judicial separation from her too complaisant old spouse, renouncing with him the greater part of her wealth.

In 1819 and later Byron dwelt at Ravenna, and indulged his love of mystery and revolt by joining the Carbonari and other secret societies. His comrades, Count Gamba and his son, also joined the revolutionary ranks, and were quickly exiled from the Papal States, and fled to Pisa. During his two years at Ravenna the poet produced " The Prophecy of Dante," " Marino Faliero," " The Blues," " Sardanapalus," " Letters on Pope," " The Two Foscari," " Cain," " The Vision of Judgment," and " Heaven and Earth."

In 1821 Byron followed his mistress and her family to Pisa, where he remained for nearly two years, occupying the Lanfranchi Palace. The Shelleys also were dwelling at Pisa at the time of his arrival. Byron conceived the idea of a new quarterly magazine, in which he and

Shelley could publish their future writings, Leigh Hunt being the editor. Hunt came over to Italy with his large family, and lived for a long time at Pisa, arranging for this strange work. Shelley concluded to do but little writing for the magazine and to accept none of its profits; and in the summer of the same year he was drowned in the Mediterranean, and thus removed forever from the scene. "The Liberal Magazine" was published for a year, but met with little success, while Byron and Hunt quarrelled incessantly.

The last Italian sojourn of the poet was at Genoa, where La Guiccioli remained in her semi-conjugal relations with him. It has been confidently stated, and quite as earnestly denied, that his affection had already begun to wane, and that the golden-haired Italian beauty had lost her charm for him. There is more certainty in the fact that he had latterly found that the public showed comparatively little interest in his new poems, and this discovery filled him with chagrin. Evidently the time had come for another great change in his life.

A noble and heroic impulse now seized this unfortunate child of genius. The cause of liberty stood then in peril in the most venerable of classic lands, and he freely gave towards its succour the purse of a wealthy man, the sword of a British peer, and the life of a transcendent genius. The provinces of Greece were then in full revolt against the despotism of Turkey, and Byron entered their service as a volunteer. Accompanied by Count Pietro Gamba, the brother of La Guiccioli, he sailed from Genoa, and after sojourning for a time at Cephalonia, with Shelley's friend Trelawney, he reached Missolonghi, a Greek city then threatened by the Turkish fleet. Here he displayed remarkable executive ability in fortifying the port, reconciling the rivalries of intriguing Greek chieftains, and holding in discipline the wild Suliote bands which composed the garrison. All manner of enthusiasts and adventurers were represented here, — volunteers from England, Italy, Germany, Sweden, America, — ambitious soldiers of fortune, visionary Philhellenes, and turbulent native troops, and the Turkish warships from time to time swooped along the coast with roaring broadsides. With lavish outlays from his private purse for the mercenary, and with fearless repressive measures for the mutinous, Byron restored his district to order and efficiency. The Greek revolutionary government had determined to test their power and risk their future by an expedition to besiege Lepanto, then in the hands of the Moslems ; and Lord Byron was appointed to the high and responsible position of commander-in-chief of this army.

But destiny robbed the hero of this glory. In the abominable climate and unhealthy conditions of Missolonghi, — a mud-bank girt about with swamps, — and himself often wet through during his long rides, his health began to break, and he became the victim of rheumatic tortures, convulsions, and fevers. Amid his fatigues and pains, however, he said: " I will stick by the cause as long as a cause exists." His medical attendance was incompetent, and treated him to profuse bleedings just when he most needed strengthening. At last inflammation of the brain set in, followed by a long lethargy. He tried in vain to frame messages for his wife, his child, and his sister. His last words were: "Now I shall go to sleep," and then, on the 19th of April, 1824, he closed his eyes forever.

Amid the profound grief of the officers and

soldiers of the Greek nation the body of Byron was laid to rest, for a time, in the church at Missolonghi, where Marco Bozzaris and other heroes had been buried. During this splendid military and ecclesiastical funeral the Greek cannon sounded thirty-seven minute-guns, — one for each year of his age, — and the dull booming of the hostile Turkish batteries came down on the wind from Patras.

When it was decided to take Byron's body back to Mother England, application was formally made for its interment in Westminster Abbey. This request was promptly refused by the Dean, and the burial took place in the family vault, not far from Newstead Abbey. Not one of the neighbouring families of nobility and gentry was represented at the obsequies.

At one time, according to Trelawney, Byron entertained hopes of becoming King of Greece, especially in view of the fact that the warring factions of that unhappy land could be united only under the firm control of a sovereign of foreign origin. He also had a desire to be appointed Greek ambassador to the United States, believing that he could influence the Great Republic to acknowledge the independence of the Hellenic nation, and that this act would be followed by similar recognitions on the part of the European powers. He had devoted much study to American topics, especially while the transatlantic artist West was leisurely painting portraits of himself and the Countess Guiccioli at Pisa. Being the most bigoted of aristocrats, he could hardly compare the new republic favourably with the older realms of Europe; but as a country of and for the people he respected it greatly, and often spoke its praises in enthusiastic terms.

He was one of the most generous of men, and always beloved even by his servants. It is said that he never lost a friend, and that his passionate susceptibilities and liberal impulses bound closely to him many men of varying characters. The prevalent gloom of his heart was usually covered with an external gayety of spirits, which made him a general favourite. And yet he was an intense aristocrat, and either as poet or peer held himself as high above the vulgar herd, distinct, unknown, and romantic.

Byron was always a sceptic, so far as regards matters of religion, without, indeed, logical and reasonable justifications, but from the force of circumstances, prejudices, and ignorance. His beloved college-companion, Matthews, was an atheist; the friend of his later years, Shelley, also stood as an unbeliever. But the latter had frequent doubts of Byron's firmness in unbelief, and stigmatized him to Trelawney as "no better than a Christian." And yet the majesty of religion and its terrors took a powerful hold upon his heart, and during the later years of his life the poet fasted rigorously on Fridays, and knelt when religious processions were passing by.

Byron showed an amiable and delightful trait in his love of animals, which began in his childhood and grew with his growth. Among his cherished pets were a bear, a wolf, several bulldogs, and the celebrated Newfoundland dog, Boatswain, which was buried at Newstead, in a vault graced by an epitaph from the poet's own hand. During his first Greek voyage, he shot an eaglet, near the Gulf of Lepanto, and suffered such deep grief for this act that he resolved never to slay a bird again.

Byron came into the world with two club feet, and both legs withered to the knee; and by an accident attending his birth the right foot received further distortion. Some partly successful attempts were made to improve these faulty members, by steel splints and otherwise, but he always remained lame and deformed, and his extreme sensitiveness in this regard cast a cloud over his entire life.

Otherwise Byron was one of the handsomest men of his time, with fine features, a colourless complexion, eyes of a light blue or grayish hue, and profuse curls of dark auburn hair. A natural tendency to corpulence he restrained by a rigid and abstemious diet, nearly starving himself to avoid grossness of figure.

The Poetical Tales were written in 1813-23, and include " The Giaour," " The Bride of Abydos," " The Corsair," " Lara," " The Siege of Corinth," " Parisina," " Mazeppa," and " The Island." They form a group of narratives of matchless force and vigour, and their novelty and originality instantly captivated the public. Indeed, it was supposed by many people that the poet himself was the hero of all these adventurous chronicles; and although this would have been impossible, yet their magnificent descriptions and wonderful episodes could not have been written unless the author had been familiar with the scenery of the classic seas, the life of the old Levantine islands and ports. Athens and the Morea, the Ægean Isles, the mountains of Albania and their picturesque inhabitants, were almost as familiar to him as his own Nottinghamshire. Therefore these tales are remarkable above all for what the moderns call " local colour,"— their definiteness, certainty, and intense vigorousness. These traits commended the stories to the people, who welcomed them with an incredible enthusiasm. The " Corsair " was written in a fortnight, in 1813, and fourteen thousand copies were sold in a single day. " Lara " came out during the following year, and met with a pronounced success.

The vices of Lord Byron were largely those of his time, an era of libertinism and sentiment, — a sentiment which was very real then but which at times seems forced and fantastic, when studied by men of the present age, with its practical and business-like tendencies, and its industrial, inventive, and commercial activities. But however archaic some of his work now seems, his masterpieces glow with the un-

INTRODUCTION.

mistakable and imperishable light of genius, and are wonderfully interpenetrated with passion and wit. The whole civilized world, from the Golden Horn to the Golden Gate, welcomed with rapture his transcendent utterances, and when he died at Missolonghi, — self-sacrificed on the altar of Freedom, — many nations mourned the departure of this wilful, wayward, dazzling soul.

M. F. SWEETSER.

THE CORSAIR.

LORD BYRON

THOMAS MOORE, Esq.

MY DEAR MOORE,—I dedicate to you the last production with which I shall trespass on public patience, and your indulgence, for some years; and I own that I feel anxious to avail myself of this latest and only opportunity of adorning my pages with a name consecrated by unshaken public principle, and the most undoubted and various talents. While Ireland ranks you among the firmest of her patriots; while you stand alone the first of her bards in her estimation, and Britain repeats and ratifies the decree, permit one whose only regret, since our first acquaintance, has been the years he had lost before it commenced, to add the humble but sincere suffrage of friendship to the voice of more than one nation. It will at least prove to you that I have neither forgotten the gratification derived from your society, nor abandoned the prospect of its renewal, whenever your leisure or inclination allows you to atone to your friends for too long an absence. It is said among those friends, I trust truly, that you are engaged in the composition of a poem whose scene will be laid in the East; none can do those scenes so much justice. The wrongs of your own country, the magnificent and fiery spirit of her sons, the beauty and feeling of her daughters, may there be found; and Collins, when he denominated his Oriental his Irish Eclogues, was not aware how true, at least, was a part of his parallel. Your imagination will create a warmer sun, and less clouded sky: but wildness, tenderness, and originality are part of your national claim of Oriental descent, to which you have already thus far proved your title more clearly than the most zealous of your country's antiquarians.

May I add a few words on a subject on which all men are supposed to be fluent, and none agreeable? — Self. I have written much, and published more than enough to demand a longer silence than I now meditate; but, for some years to come, it is my intention to tempt no further the award of "gods, men, nor columns." In the present composition I have attempted not the most difficult, but perhaps the best adapted measure to our language, the good old and now neglected heroic couplet. The stanza of Spenser is perhaps too slow and dignified for narrative; though, I confess, it is the measure most after my own heart. Scott alone, of the present generation, has hitherto completely triumphed over the fatal facility of the octo-syllabic verse; and this is not the least victory of his fertile and mighty genius. In blank verse, Milton, Thomson, and our dramatists, are the beacons that shine along the deep, but warn us from the rough and barren rock on which they are kindled. The heroic couplet is not the most popular measure, certainly: but as I did not deviate into the other from a wish to flatter what is called public opinion, I shall quit it without further apology, and take my chance once more with that versification in which I have hitherto published nothing but compositions whose former circulation is part of my present, and will be of my future regret.

With regard to my story, and stories in

general, I should have been glad to have rendered my personages more perfect and amiable, if possible, inasmuch as I have been sometimes criticised, and considered no less responsible for their deeds and qualities than if all had been personal. Be it so. If I have deviated into the gloomy vanity of "drawing from self," the pictures are probably like, since they are unfavourable; and if not, those who know me are undeceived, and those who do not, I have little interest in undeceiving. I have no particular desire that any but my acquaintance should think the author better than the beings of his imagining; but I cannot help a little surprise, and perhaps amusement, at some odd critical exceptions in the present instance, when I see several bards (far more deserving, I allow), in very reputable plight, and quite exempted from all participation in the faults of those heroes, who, nevertheless, might be found with little more morality than "The Giaour," and perhaps — but no — I must admit Childe Harold to be a very repulsive personage; and as to his identity, those who like it must give him whatever *alias* they please.

If, however, it were worth while to remove

the impression, it might be of some service to
me, that the man who is alike the delight of his
readers and his friends, the poet of all circles,
and the idol of his own, permits me here and
elsewhere to subscribe myself, most truly and
affectionately, his obedient servant,

BYRON.

January 2, 1814.

THE CORSAIR.

CANTO THE FIRST.

"—————— nessun maggior dolore,
Che ricordarsi del tempo felice
Nella miseria, ———."   DANTE.

I.

" O'ER the glad waters of the dark-blue sea,*
Our thoughts as boundless, and our souls as free,
Far as the breeze can bear, the billows foam,
Survey our empire, and behold our home !
These are our realms, no limits to their sway —
Our flag the sceptre all who meet obey.

* The time in this poem may seem too short for the occurrences, but the whole of the Ægean isles are within a few hours' sail of the continent, and the reader must be kind enough to take the *wind* as I have often found it.

THE CORSAIR.

Ours the wild life in tumult still to range,
From toil to rest, and joy in every change.
Oh, who can tell? not thou, luxurious slave!
Whose soul would sicken o'er the heaving wave;
Not thou, vain lord of wantonness and ease!
Whom slumber soothes not — pleasure cannot please —
Oh, who can tell, save he whose heart hath tried,
And danced in triumph o'er the waters wide,
The exulting sense — the pulse's maddening play,
That thrills the wanderer of that trackless way?
That for itself can woo the approaching fight,
And turn what some deem danger to delight;
That seeks what cravens shun with more than zeal,
And where the feebler faint — can only feel —
Feel — to the rising bosom's inmost core,
Its hope awaken and its spirit soar?
No dread of death — if with us die our foes —
Save that it seems even duller than repose:
Come when it will — we snatch the life of life —
When lost — what recks it — by disease or strife?
Let him who crawls enamour'd of decay,
Cling to his couch, and sicken years away;
Heave his thick breath, and shake his palsied head;
Ours — the fresh turf, and not the feverish bed.
While gasp by gasp he falters forth his soul,
Ours with one pang — one bound — escapes control.
His corse may boast its urn and narrow cave,
And they who loathed his life may gild his grave;

Ours are the tears, though few, sincerely shed,
When Ocean shrouds and sepulchres our dead.
For us, even banquets fond regret supply
In the red cup that crowns our memory:
And the brief epitaph in danger's day,
When those who win at length divide the prey,
And cry, Remembrance saddening o'er each brow,
How had the brave who fell exulted *now!*"

II.

Such were the notes that from the Pirate's isle,
Around the kindling watch-fire rang the while;
Such were the sounds that thrill'd the rocks along,
And unto ears as rugged seem'd a song!
In scatter'd groups upon the golden sand,
They game — carouse — converse — or whet the brand;
Select the arms — to each his blade assign,
And careless eye the blood that dims its shine;
Repair the boat, replace the helm or oar,
While others straggling muse along the shore;
For the wild bird the busy springes set,
Or spread beneath the sun the dripping net;
Gaze where some distant sail a speck supplies,
With all the thirsting eye of Enterprise;
Tell o'er the tales of many a night of toil,
And marvel where they next shall seize a spoil:
No matter where — their chief's allotment this;
Theirs, to believe no prey nor plan amiss.

But who that CHIEF? his name on every shore
Is famed and fear'd — they ask and know no more.
With these he mingles not but to command ;
Few are his words, but keen his eye and hand.
Ne'er seasons he with mirth their jovial mess,
But they forgive his silence for success.
Ne'er for his lip the purpling cup they fill,
That goblet passes him untasted still —
And for his fare — the rudest of his crew
Would that, in turn, have pass'd untasted too :
Earth's coarsest bread, the garden's homeliest roots,
And scarce the summer luxury of fruits,
His short repast in humbleness supply
With all a hermit's board would scarce deny.
But while he shuns the grosser joys of sense,
His mind seems nourish'd by that abstinence.
"Steer to that shore!" — they sail. "Do this!"
    — 't is done!
"Now form and follow me!" — the spoil is won.
Thus prompt his accents and his actions still,
And all obey and few inquire his will ;
To such, brief answer and contemptuous eye
Convey reproof, nor further deign reply.

"A sail! — a sail!" — a promised prize to Hope!
Her nation — flag — how speaks the telescope?
No prize, alas! but yet a welcome sail :
The blood-red signal glitters in the gale.

THE CORSAIR.

Yes — she is ours — a home returning bark —
Blow fair, thou breeze ! — she anchors ere the dark.
Already doubled is the cape — our bay
Receives that prow which proudly spurns the spray.
How gloriously her gallant course she goes !
Her white wings flying — never from her foes —
She walks the waters like a thing of life,
And seems to dare the elements to strife.
Who would not brave the battle-fire — the wreck —
To move the monarch of her peopled deck ?

Hoarse o'er her side the rustling cable rings ;
The sails are furl'd ; and anchoring, round she
    swings ;
And gathering loiterers on the land discern
Her boat descending from the latticed stern.
'T is mann'd — the oars keep concert to the strand
Till grates her keel upon the shallow sand.
Hail to the welcome shout ! — the friendly speech !
When hand grasps hand uniting on the beach :
The smile, the question, and the quick reply,
And the heart's promise of festivity !

The tidings spread, and gathering grows the crowd :
The hum of voices, and the laughter loud,
And woman's gentler anxious tone is heard —

Friends' — husbands' — lovers' names in each dear
    word :
" Oh ! are they safe ? we ask not of success ,
But shall we see them ? will their accents bless?
From where the battle roars, the billows chafe,
They doubtless boldly did — but who are safe?
Here let them haste to gladden and surprise,
And kiss the doubt from these delighted eyes !"

VI.

" Where is our chief? for him we bear report —
And doubt that joy — which hails our coming —
    short ;
Yet thus sincere — 't is cheering, though so brief ;
But, Juan ! instant guide us to our chief :
Our greeting paid, we 'll feast on our return,
And all shall hear what each may wish to learn."
Ascending slowly by the rock-hewn way,
To where his watch-tower beetles o'er the bay
By bushy brake, and wild flowers blossoming,
And freshness breathing from each silver spring,
Whose scatter'd streams from granite basins burst,
Leap into life, and sparkling woo your thirst ;
From crag to cliff they mount. — Near yonder
    cave,
What lonely straggler looks along the wave ?
In pensive posture leaning on the brand,
Not oft a resting-staff to that red hand ?
" 'T is he — 't is Conrad — here, as wont — alone ;

On — Juan! — on — and make our purpose known.
The bark he views — and tell him we would greet
His ear with tidings he must quickly meet:
We dare not yet approach — thou know'st his mood,
When strange or uninvited steps intrude."

Him Juan sought, and told of their intent:
He spake not, but a sign express'd assent.
These Juan calls — they come — to their salute
He bends him slightly, but his lips are mute.
"These letters, Chief, are from the Greek — the spy,
Who still proclaims our spoil or peril nigh:
Whate'er his tidings, we can well report
Much that" — " Peace, peace!" — he cuts their prating short.
Wondering they turn, abash'd, while each to each
Conjecture whispers in his muttering speech:
They watch his glance with many a stealing look,
To gather how that eye the tidings took;
But, this as if he guess'd, with head aside,
Perchance from some emotion, doubt, or pride,
He read the scroll — "My tablets, Juan, hark —
Where is Gonsalvo?"
" In the anchor'd bark."
"There let him stay — to him this order bear.
Back to your duty — for my course prepare:

Myself this enterprise to-night will share."
"To-night, Lord Conrad?"
                              "Ay! at set of sun:
The breeze will freshen when the day is done.
My corslet — cloak — one hour and we are gone.
Sling on thy bugle — see that free from rust
My carbine-lock springs worthy of my trust;
Be the edge sharpen'd of my boarding-brand,
And give its guard more room to fit my hand.
This let the armourer with speed dispose;
Last time, it more fatigued my arm than foes:
Mark that the signal-gun be duly fired,
To tell us when the hour of stay's expired."

VIII.

They make obeisance, and retire in haste,
Too soon to seek again the watery waste:
Yet they repine not — so that Conrad guides;
And who dare question aught that he decides?
That man of loneliness and mystery,
Scarce seen to smile, and seldom heard to sigh;
Whose name appals the fiercest of his crew,
And tints each swarthy cheek with sallower hue;
Still sways their souls with that commanding art
That dazzles, leads, yet chills the vulgar heart.
What is that spell, that thus his lawless train
Confess and envy, yet oppose in vain?
What should it be, that thus their faith can bind?
The power of Thought — the magic of the Mind!

Link'd with success, assumed and kept with skill,
That moulds another's weakness to its will;
Wields with their hands, but, still to these unknown,
Makes even their mightiest deeds appear his own.
Such hath it been — shall be: beneath the sun
The many still must labour for the one!
'T is nature's doom — but let the wretch who toils,
Accuse not, hate not *him* who wears the spoils.
Oh! if he knew the weight of splendid chains,
How light the balance of his humbler pains!

IX.

Unlike the heroes of each ancient race,
Demons in act, but gods at least in face,
In Conrad's form seems little to admire,
Though his dark eyebrow shades a glance of fire:
Robust but not Herculean — to the sight
No giant frame sets forth his common height;
Yet, in the whole, who paused to look again,
Saw more than marks the crowd of vulgar men;
They gaze and marvel how — and still confess
That thus it is, but why they cannot guess.
Sun-burnt his cheek, his forehead high and pale
The sable curls in wild profusion veil;
And oft perforce his rising lip reveals
The haughtier thought it curbs, but scarce conceals.
Though smooth his voice, and calm his general mien,

Still seems there something he would not have
    seen;
His features' deepening lines and varying hue
At times attracted, yet perplex'd the view,
As if within that murkiness of mind
Work'd feelings fearful, and yet undefined;
Such might it be — that none could truly tell —
Too close inquiry his stern glance would quell.
There breathe but few whose aspect might defy
The full encounter of his searching eye;
He had the skill, when Cunning's gaze would seek
To probe his heart and watch his changing cheek,
At once the observer's purpose to espy,
And on himself roll back his scrutiny,
Lest he to Conrad rather should betray
Some secret thought, than drag that chief's to day.
There was a laughing devil in his sneer,
That raised emotions both of rage and fear;
And where his frown of hatred darkly fell,
Hope withering fled, and Mercy sigh'd farewell!

x.

Slight are the outward signs of evil thought,
Within — within — 't was there the spirit wrought!
Love shows all changes: Hate, Ambition, Guile,
Betray no further than the bitter smile:
The lip's least curl, the lightest paleness thrown
Along the govern'd aspect, speak alone
Of deeper passions, and to judge their mien,

He who would see, must be himself unseen.
Then — with the hurried tread, the upward eye,
The clenched hand, the pause of agony,
That listens, starting, lest the step too near
Approach intrusive on that mood of fear:
Then — with each feature working from the heart,
With feelings loosed to strengthen — not depart:
That rise, convulse, contend — that freeze, or glow,
Flush in the cheek, or damp upon the brow;
Then, Stranger, if thou canst, and tremblest not,
Behold his soul — the rest that soothes his lot!
Mark how that lone and blighted bosom sears
The scathing thought of execrated years!
Behold — but who hath seen, or e'er shall see,
Man as himself — the secret spirit free?

XI.

Yet was not Conrad thus by Nature sent
To lead the guilty — guilt's worst instrument:
His soul was changed, before his deeds had driven
Him forth to war with man and forfeit heaven.
Warp'd by the world in Disappointment's school,
In words too wise, in conduct *there* a fool;
Too firm to yield, and far too proud to stoop,
Doom'd by his very virtues for a dupe,
He cursed those virtues as the cause of ill,
And not the traitors who betray'd him still;
Nor deem'd that gifts bestow'd on better men
Had left him joy and means to give again.

Fear'd, shunn'd, belied, ere youth had lost her
    force,
He hated man too much to feel remorse,
And thought the voice of wrath a sacred call,
To pay the injuries of some on all.
He knew himself a villain, but he deem'd
The rest no better than the thing he seem'd;
And scorn'd the best as hypocrites who hid
Those deeds the bolder spirit plainly did.
He knew himself detested, but he knew
The hearts that loathed him, crouch'd and dreaded
    too
Lone, wild, and strange, he stood alike exempt
From all affection and from all contempt:
His name could sadden, and his acts surprise;
But they that fear'd him dared not to despise.
Man spurns the worm, but pauses ere he wake
The slumbering venom of the folded snake:
The first may turn, but not avenge the blow;
The last expires, but leaves no living foe;
Fast to the doom'd offender's form it clings,
And he may crush — not conquer — still it stings!

XII.

None are all evil; quickening round his heart,
One softer feeling would not yet depart:
Oft could he sneer at others, as beguiled
By passions worthy of a fool or child;
Yet 'gainst that passion vainly still he strove,

And even in him it asks the name of Love!
Yes, it was love — unchangeable — unchanged,
Felt but for one from whom he never ranged;
Though fairest captives daily met his eye,
He shunn'd, nor sought, but coldly pass'd them by:
Though many a beauty droop'd in prison'd bower,
None ever soothed his most unguarded hour.
Yes — it was Love — if thoughts of tenderness,
Tried in temptation, strengthen'd by distress,
Unmoved by absence, firm in every clime,
And yet — oh, more than all! — untired by time;
Which nor defeated hope, nor baffled wile,
Could render sullen were she near to smile,
Nor rage could fire, nor sickness fret to vent
On her one murmur of his discontent;
Which still would meet with joy, with calmness
    part,
Lest that his look of grief should reach her heart:
Which naught removed, nor menaced to remove —
If there be love in mortals — this was love!
He was a villain — ay, reproaches shower
On him — but not the passion, nor its power,
Which only proved, all other virtues gone,
Nor guilt itself could quench this loveliest one!

He paused a moment — till his hastening men
Pass'd the first winding downward to the glen.
" Strange tidings! — many a peril have I past,

Nor know I why this next appears the last!
Yet so my heart forebodes, but must not fear,
Nor shall my followers find me falter here.
'T is rash to meet, but surer death to wait
Till here they hunt us to undoubted fate ;
And if my plan but hold, and Fortune smile,
We 'll furnish mourners for our funeral pile.
Ay, let them slumber — peaceful be their dreams !
Morn ne'er awoke them with such brilliant beams
As kindle high to-night (but blow, thou breeze!)
To warn these slow avengers of the seas.
Now to Medora — Oh ! my sinking heart,
Long may her own be lighter than thou art :
Yet was I brave — mean boast where all are brave !
Even insects sting for aught they seek to save.
This common courage which with brutes we share
That owes its deadliest efforts to despair,
Small merit claims ; but 't was my nobler hope
To teach my few with numbers still to cope.
Long have I led them — not to vainly bleed :
No medium now — we perish or succeed !
So let it be — it irks not me to die ;
But thus to urge them whence they cannot fly.
My lot hath long had little of my care,
But chafes my pride thus baffled in the snare :
Is this my skill? my craft ? to set at last
Hope, power, and life upon a single cast ?
Oh, Fate ! — accuse thy folly, not thy fate ;
She may redeem thee still — nor yet too late."

Thus with himself communion held he, till
He reach'd the summit of his tower-crown'd hill:
There at the portal paused — for wild and soft
He heard those accents never heard too oft;
Through the high lattice far yet sweet they rung,
And these the notes his bird of beauty sung:

" Deep in my soul that tender secret dwells,
    Lonely and lost to light for evermore,
Save when to thine my heart responsive swells,
    Then trembles into silence as before.

" There, in its centre, a sepulchral lamp
    Burns the slow flame, eternal, — but unseen;
Which not the darkness of despair can damp,
    Though vain its ray as it had never been.

" Remember me — Oh! pass not thou my grave
    Without one thought whose relics there recline:
The only pang my bosom dare not brave
    Must be to find forgetfulness in thine.

" My fondest — faintest — latest accents hear:
    Grief for the dead not virtue can reprove;
Then give me all I ever ask'd — a tear,
    The first — last — sole reward of so much love!"

He pass'd the portal — cross'd the corridore,
And reach'd the chamber as the strain gave o'er:
" My own Medora! — sure thy song is sad — "

" In Conrad's absence wouldst thou have it glad?
Without thine ear to listen to my lay,
Still must my song my thoughts, my soul betray :
Still must each accent to my bosom suit,
My heart unhush'd — although my lips were mute!
Oh! many a night on this lone couch reclined,
My dreaming fear with storms hath wing'd the
    wind,
And deem'd the breath that faintly fann'd thy sail
The murmuring prelude of the ruder gale ;
Though soft, it seem'd the low prophetic dirge,
That mourn'd thee floating on the savage surge:
Still would I rise to rouse the beacon fire.
Lest spies less true should let the blaze expire ;
And many a restless hour outwatch'd each star,
And morning came — and still thou wert afar.
Oh ! how the chill blast on my bosom blew,
And day broke dreary on my troubled view,
And still I gazed and gazed — and not a prow
Was granted to my tears, my truth, my vow !
At length — 't was noon — I hail'd and blest the
    mast
That met my sight — it near'd — Alas, it pass'd !
Another came — O God ! 't was thine at last !
Would that those days were over ! wilt thou ne'er.
My Conrad, learn the joys of peace to share?
Sure thou hast more than wealth, and many a home
As bright as this invites us not to roam ;
Thou know'st it is not peril that I fear,

I only tremble when thou art not here;
Then not for mine, but that far dearer life,
Which flies from love and languishes for strife —
How strange that heart, to me so tender still,
Should war with nature and its better will!"

"Yea, strange indeed — that heart hath long been
    changed;
Worm-like 't was trampled — adder-like avenged,
Without one hope on earth beyond thy love,
And scarce a glimpse of mercy from above.
Yet the same feeling which thou dost condemn,
My very love to thee is hate to them,
So closely mingling here, that disentwined,
I cease to love thee when I love mankind:
Yet dread not this — the proof of all the past
Assures the future that my love will last;
But — O Medora! nerve thy gentler heart,
This hour again — but not for long — we part."
"This hour we part! — my heart foreboded this!
Thus ever fade my fairy dreams of bliss.
This hour — it cannot be — this hour away!
Yon bark hath hardly anchor'd in the bay:
Her consort still is absent, and her crew
Have need of rest before they toil anew:
My love! thou mock'st my weakness, and wouldst
    steel
My breast before the time when it must feel;
But trifle now no more with my distress,

Such mirth hath less of play than bitterness.
Be silent, Conrad! — dearest! come and share
The feast these hands delighted to prepare;
Light toil! to cull and dress thy frugal fare!
See, I have pluck'd the fruit that promised best,
And where not sure, perplex'd, but pleased, I guess'd
At such as seem'd the fairest: thrice the hill
My steps have wound to try the coolest rill;
Yes! thy sherbet to-night will sweetly flow,
See how it sparkles in its vase of snow!
The grape's gay juice thy bosom never cheers;
Thou more than Moslem when the cup appears:
Think not I mean to chide — for I rejoice
What others deem a penance is thy choice.
But come, the board is spread; our silver lamp
Is trimm'd, and heeds not the Sirocco's damp
Then shall my handmaids while the time along,
And join with me the dance, or wake the song;
Or my guitar, which still thou lov'st to hear,
Shall soothe or lull; — or, should it vex thine ear,
We 'll turn the tale, by Ariosto told,
Of fair Olympia loved and left of old.*
Why — thou wert worse than he who broke his vow
To that lost damsel, shouldst thou leave me now;
Or-even that traitor chief — I 've seen thee smile,
When the clear sky show'd Ariadne's Isle,
Which I have pointed from these cliffs the while:
And thus, half sportive, half in fear, I said,

* *Orlando Furioso*, Canto 10.

. . . Her long fair hair lay floating
o'er his arms,
In all the wildness of dishevell'd
charms. . . .

Lest time should raise that doubt to more than dread,
Thus Conrad, too, will quit me for the main:
And he deceived me — for — he came again!"

" Again — again — and oft again, my love !
If there be life below, and hope above,
He will return — but now the moments bring
The time of parting with redoubled wing:
The why — the where — what boots it now to tell?
Since all must end in that wild word — farewell!
Yet would I fain — did time allow — disclose —
Fear not — these are no formidable foes ;
And here shall watch a more than wonted guard,
For sudden siege and long defence prepared :
Nor be thou lonely — though thy lord's away,
Our matrons and thy handmaids with thee stay :
And this thy comfort — that when next we meet,
Security shall make repose more sweet.
List ! — 't is the bugle" — Juan shrilly blew —
" One kiss — one more — another — Oh! Adieu! "
She rose, she sprung, she clung to his embrace,
Till his heart heaved beneath her hidden face,
He dared not raise to his that deep-blue eye,
Which downcast droop'd in tearless agony.
Her long fair hair lay floating o'er his arms,
In all the wildness of dishevell'd charms ;
Scarce beat that bosom where his image dwelt
So full — *that* feeling seem'd almost unfelt !
Hark — peals the thunder of the signal-gun !

It told 't was sunset — and he cursed that sun.
Again — again — that form he madly press'd,
Which mutely clasp'd, imploringly caress'd !
And tottering to the couch his bride he bore ;
One moment gazed, as if to gaze no more ;
Felt that for him earth held but her alone,
Kiss'd her cold forehead — turn'd — is Conrad gone?

XV.

" And is he gone ? " — on sudden solitude
How oft that fearful question will intrude !
" 'T was but an instant past — and here he stood !
And now " — without the portal's porch she rush'd
And then at length her tears in freedom gush'd :
Big, bright, and fast, unknown to her they fell ;
But still her lips refused to send — " Farewell ! "
For in that word, that fatal word — howe'er
We promise, hope, believe — there breathes despair.
O'er every feature of that still, pale face,
Had sorrow fix'd what time can ne'er erase :
The tender blue of that large loving eye
Grew frozen with its gaze on vacancy.
Till — oh, how far ! — it caught a glimpse of him,
And then it flow'd, and frenzied seem'd to swim,
Through those long, dark, and glistening lashes dew'd
With drops of sadness oft to be renew'd.
" He 's gone ! " — against her heart that hand is driven,

Convulsed and quick — then gently raised to
    heaven;
She look'd, and saw the heaving of the main;
The white sail set — she dared not look again;
But turn'd with sickening soul within the gate —
" It is no dream — and I am desolate! "

From crag to crag descending, swiftly sped
Stern Conrad down, nor once he turned his head;
But shrunk whene'er the windings of his way
Forced on his eye what he would not survey —
His lone but lovely dwelling on the steep,
That hail'd him first when homeward from the
    deep:
And she — the dim and melancholy star,
Whose ray of beauty reach'd him from afar,
On her he must not gaze, he must not think,
There he might rest — but on Destruction's brink:
Yet once almost he stopp'd, and nearly gave
His fate to chance, his projects to the wave;
But no — it must not be — a worthy chief
May melt, but not betray to woman's grief.
He sees his bark, he notes how fair the wind,
And sternly gathers all his might of mind:
Again he hurries on; and as he hears
The clang of tumult vibrate on his ears,
The busy sounds, the bustle of the shore,

The shout, the signal, and the dashing oar;
As marks his eye the seaboy on the mast,
The anchors rise, the sails unfurling fast,
The waving kerchiefs of the crowd that urge
That mute adieu to those who stem the surge;
And more than all, his blood-red flag aloft,
He marvell'd how his heart could seem so soft.
Fire in his glance, and wildness in his breast,
He feels of all his former self possest;
He bounds — he flies — until his footsteps reach
The verge where ends the cliff, begins the beach,
There checks his speed; but pauses less to breathe
The breezy freshness of the deep beneath,
Than there his wonted statelier step renew;
Nor rush, disturb'd by haste, to vulgar view:
For well had Conrad learn'd to curb the crowd,
By arts that veil, and oft preserve the proud:
His was the lofty port, the distant mien,
That seems to shun the sight — and awes if seen:
The solemn aspect, and the high-born eye,
That checks low mirth, but lacks not courtesy;
All these he wielded to command assent:
But where he wish'd to win, so well unbent,
That kindness cancell'd fear in those who heard,
And others' gifts show'd mean beside his word,
When echo'd to the heart as from his own
His deep yet tender melody of tone:
But such was foreign to his wonted mood,
He cared not what he soften'd, but subdued;

The evil passions of his youth had made
Him value less who loved — than what obey'd.

XVII.

Around him mustering ranged his ready guard,
Before him Juan stands — " Are all prepar'd?"
"They are — nay, more — embark'd: the latest boat
Waits but my chief —— "
    " My sword and my capote."
Soon firmly girded on, and lightly slung,
His belt and cloak were o'er his shoulders flung:
"Call Pedro here" — He comes — and Conrad bends
With all the courtesy he deign'd his friends:
" Receive these tablets, and peruse with care,
Words of high trust and truth are graven there ;
Double the guard, and when Anselmo's bark
Arrives, let him alike these orders mark:
In three days (serve the breeze) the sun shall shine
On our return — till then all peace be thine!"
This said, his brother pirate's hand he wrung,
Then to his boat with haughty gesture sprung.
Flash'd the dipt oars, and sparkling with the stroke,
Around the waves' phosphoric * brightness broke :
They gain the vessel — on the deck he stands —

* By night, particularly in a warm latitude, every stroke of the oar, every motion of the boat or ship, is followed by a slight flash like sheet-lightning from the water.

Shrieks the shrill whistle — ply the busy hands:
He marks how well the ship her helm obeys,
How gallant all her crew — and deigns to praise.
His eyes of pride to young Gonsalvo turn —
Why doth he start, and inly seem to mourn?
Alas! those eyes beheld his rocky tower,
And live a moment o'er the parting hour;
She — his Medora — did she mark the prow?
Ah! never loved he half so much as now!
But much must yet be done ere dawn of day —
Again he mans himself and turns away;
Down to the cabin with Gonsalvo bends,
And there unfolds his plan — his means — and ends;
Before them burns the lamp, and spreads the chart,
And all that speaks and aids the naval art:
They to the midnight watch protract debate;
To anxious eyes what hour is ever late?
Meantime the steady breeze serenely blew,
And fast and falcon-like the vessel flew;
Pass'd the high headlands of each clustering isle,
To gain their port — long — long ere morning smile:
And soon the night-glass through the narrow bay
Discovers where the Pacha's galleys lay.
Count they each sail, and mark how there supine
The lights in vain o'er heedless Moslem shine.
Secure, unnoted, Conrad's prow pass'd by,
And anchor'd where his ambush meant to lie;

THE CORSAIR.

Screen'd from espial by the jutting cape,
That rears on high its rude fantastic shape.
Then rose his band to duty — not from sleep —
Equipp'd for deeds alike on land or deep;
While lean'd their leader o'er the fretting flood,
And calmly talk'd — and yet he talk'd of blood!

CANTO THE SECOND.

"Conosceste i dubiosi desiri?"— DANTE.

I.

IN Coron's bay floats many a galley light,
Through Coron's lattices the lamps are bright,
For Seyd, the Pacha, makes a feast to-night:
A feast for promis'd triumph yet to come,
When he shall drag the fetter'd Rovers home.
This hath he sworn by Alla and his sword;
And faithful to his firman and his word,
His summon'd prows collect along the coast,
And great the gathering crews, and loud the boast;
Already shared the captives and the prize,
Though far the distant foe they thus despise;
'T is but to sail — no doubt to-morrow's sun
Will see the Pirates bound — their haven won!

THE CORSAIR.   29

Meantime the watch may slumber, if they will,
Nor only wake to war, but dreaming kill.
Though all, who can, disperse on shore and seek
To flesh their glowing valour on the Greek;
How well such deed becomes the turban'd brave,
To bare the sabre's edge before a slave!
Infest his dwelling — but forbear to slay,
Their arms are strong, yet merciful to-day,
And do not deign to smite because they may!
Unless some gay caprice suggests the blow,
To keep in practice for the coming foe.
Revel and rout the evening hours beguile,
And they who wish to wear a head must smile;
For Moslem mouths produce their choicest cheer,
And hoard their curses, till the coast is clear.

High in his hall reclines the turban'd Seyd;
Around — the bearded chiefs he came to lead.
Removed the banquet, and the last pilaff —
Forbidden draughts, 't is said, he dared to quaff,
Though to the rest the sober berry's juice,*
The slaves bear round for rigid Moslems' use;
The long chibouques † dissolving cloud supply,
While dance the Almas ‡ to wild minstrelsy.
The rising morn will view the chiefs embark;
But waves are somewhat treacherous in the dark;

* Coffee.   † Pipe.   ‡ Dancing girls.

And revellers may more securely sleep
On silken couch than o'er the rugged deep;
Feast there who can — nor combat till they must,
And less to conquest than to Korans trust;
And yet the numbers crowded in his host
Might warrant more than even the Pacha's boast.

III.

With cautious reverence from the outer gate,
Slow stalks the slave, whose office there to wait,
Bows his bent head, his hand salutes the floor,
Ere yet his tongue the trusted tidings bore :
" A captive Dervise, from the Pirate's nest
Escaped, is here — himself would tell the rest." *

* It has been objected that Conrad's entering disguised as a spy is out of nature :— perhaps so. I find something not unlike it in history.

" Anxious to explore with his own eyes the state of the Vandals, Majorian ventured, after disguising the colour of his hair, to visit Carthage in the character of his own ambassador; and Genseric was afterwards mortified by the discovery that he had entertained and dismissed the Emperor of the Romans. Such an anecdote may be rejected as an improbable fiction; but it is a fiction which would not have been imagined unless in the life of a hero."— GIBBON, *Decline and Fall*, vol. vi., p. 180.

That Conrad is a character not altogether out of nature, I shall attempt to prove by some historical coincidences which I have met with since writing *The Corsair*.

" Eccelin prisonnier," dit Rolandini, " s'enfermoit dans un silence menaçant, il fixoit sur la terre son visage féroce,

He took the sign from Seyd's assenting eye,
And led the holy man in silence nigh.
His arms were folded on his dark-green vest,
His step was feeble, and his look depressed ;
Yet worn he seemed of hardship more than years,
And pale his cheek with penance, not from fears.
Vow'd to his God — his sable locks he wore,
And these his lofty cap rose proudly o'er ;
Around his form his loose long robe was thrown,
And wrapt a breast bestow'd on Heaven alone ;
Submissive, yet with self-possession mann'd,
He calmly met the curious eyes that scann'd ;
And question of his coming fain would seek,
Before the Pacha's will allow'd to speak.

et ne donnoit point d'essor à sa profonde indignation. — De toutes parts cependant les soldats et les peuples accouroient ; ils vouloient voir cet homme, jadis si puissant, et la joie universelle éclatoit de toutes parts. . . Eccelin étoit d'une petite taille ; mais tout l'aspect de sa personne, tous ses mouvemens, indiquoient un soldat. — Son langage étoit amer, son déportement superbe — et par son seul égard, il faisoit trembler les plus hardis." — SISMONDI, tome iii., pp., 219, 220.

"Gizericus (Genseric, king of the Vandals, the conqueror of both Carthage and Rome), staturâ mediocris, et equi casu claudicans, animo profundus, sermone rarus, luxuriæ contemptor, irâ turbidus, habendi cupidus, ad solicitandas gentes providentissimus," &c. &c. — JORNANDES, *de Rebus Geticis*, c. 33.

I beg leave to quote these gloomy realities to keep in countenance my Giaour and Corsair.

" Whence com'st thou, Dervise ? "
                              " From the outlaw's den
A fugitive — "
                    " Thy capture where and when ? "
" From Scalanovo's port to Scio's isle,
The Saick was bound ; but Alla did not smile
Upon our course — the Moslem merchant's gains
The Rovers won : our limbs have worn their chains.
I had no death to fear, nor wealth to boast,
Beyond the wandering freedom which I lost ;
At length a fisher's humble boat by night
Afforded hope, and offer'd chance of flight :
I seized the hour, and find my safety here ;
With thee, most mighty Pacha ! who can fear ? "

" How speed the outlaws ? stand they well prepared
Their plunder'd wealth, and robber's rock to guard ?
Dream they of this our preparation, doom'd
To view with fire their scorpion nest consumed ? "

" Pacha ! the fetter'd captive's mourning eye,
That weeps for flight, but ill can play the spy ·
I only heard the reckless waters roar,
Those waves that would not bear me from the shore ;
I only mark'd the glorious sun and sky,
Too bright — too blue — for my captivity ;

And felt — that all which Freedom's bosom cheers,
Must break my chain before it dried my tears.
This may'st thou judge, at least, from my escape,
They little deem of aught in peril's shape ;
Else vainly had I pray'd or sought the chance
That leads me here — if eyed with vigilance ;
The careless guard that did not see me fly,
May watch as idly when thy power is nigh.
Pacha ! — my limbs are faint — and nature craves
Food for my hunger, rest from tossing waves :
Permit my absence — peace be with thee ! — Peace
With all around ! — now grant repose — release."

" Stay, Dervise ! I have more to question — stay,
I do command thee — sit — dost hear ? — obey !
More I must ask, and food the slaves shall bring ;
Thou shalt not pine where all are banqueting :
The supper done — prepare thee to reply,
Clearly and full — I love not mystery."
'T were vain to guess what shook the pious man,
Who look'd not lovingly on that Divan ;
Nor show'd high relish for a banquet prest,
And less respect for every fellow-guest.
'T was but a moment's peevish hectic past
Along his cheek, and tranquillized as fast :
He sate him down in silence, and his look
Resumed the calmness which before forsook :
The feast was usher'd in ; but sumptuous fare
He shunn'd as if some poison mingled there.

For one so long condemn'd to toil and fast,
Methinks he strangely spares the rich repast.
"What ails thee, Dervise? eat — dost thou suppose
This feast a Christian's? or my friends thy foes?
Why dost thou shun the salt? that sacred pledge,
Which, once partaken, blunts the sabre's edge,
Makes even contending tribes in peace unite,
And hated hosts seem brethren to the sight!"

"Salt seasons dainties — and my food is still
The humblest root, my drink the simplest rill;
And my stern vow and order's * laws oppose
To break or mingle bread with friends or foes :
It may seem strange — if there be aught to dread,
That peril rests upon my single head;
But for thy sway — nay more — thy Sultan's throne,
I taste nor bread nor banquet — save alone;
Infringed our order's rule, the Prophet's rage
To Mecca's dome might bar my pilgrimage."

"Well — as thou wilt — ascetic as thou art —
One question answer; then in peace depart.
How many? — Ha! it cannot sure be day?
What star — what sun is bursting on the bay?
It shines a lake of fire! — away — away!
Ho! treachery! my guards! my scimitar!
The galleys feed the flames — and I afar!

* The dervises are in colleges and of different orders, as the monks.

Accursèd Dervise! — these thy tidings — thou
Some villain spy — seize — cleave him — slay him
   now!"

Up rose the Dervise with that burst of light,
Nor less his change of form appall'd the sight;
Up rose that Dervise — not in saintly garb,
But like a warrior bounding on his barb,
Dash'd his high cap, and tore his robe away —
Shone his mail'd breast, and flash'd his sabre's
   ray!
His close but glittering casque, and sable plume,
More glittering eye, and black brow's sabler gloom
Glared on the Moslems' eyes some Afrit sprite,
Whose demon death-blow left no hope for fight.
The wild confusion, and the swarthy glow
Of flames on high, and torches from below;
The shriek of terror, and the mingling yell —
For swords began to clash, and shouts to swell,
Flung o'er that spot of earth the air of hell!
Distracted, to and fro, the flying slaves
Behold but bloody shore and fiery waves;
Nought heeded they the Pacha's angry cry,
They seize that Dervise! — seize on Zatanai! *
He saw their terror — check'd the first despair
That urged him but to stand and perish there,
Since far too early and too well obey'd,
The flame was kindled ere the signal made;

       * Satan.

He saw their terror — from his baldric drew
His bugle — brief the blast — but shrilly blew:
'T is answered — " Well ye speed, my gallant crew !
Why did I doubt their quickness of career,
And deem design had left me single here?"
Sweeps his long arm — that sabre's whirling sway
Sheds fast atonement for its first delay;
Completes his fury what their fear begun,
And makes the many basely quail to one.
The cloven turbans o'er the chamber spread,
And scarce an arm dare rise to guard its head:
Even Seyd, convulsed, o'erwhelm'd with rage, surprise,
Retreats before him, though he still defies.
No craven he — and yet he dreads the blow,
So much Confusion magnifies his foe !
His blazing galleys still distract his sight,
He tore his beard, and foaming fled the fight;
For now the pirates pass'd the Haram gate,
And burst within — and it were death to wait;
Where wild Amazement shrieking — kneeling — throws
The sword aside — in vain — the blood o'erflows!
The corsairs pouring, haste to where within,
Invited Conrad's bugle, and the din
Of groaning victims, and wild cries for life,
Proclaim'd how well he did the work of strife.
They shout to find him grim and lonely there,
A glutted tiger mangling in his lair !

THE CORSAIR.   37

But short their greeting, shorter his reply —
" 'T is well — but Seyd escapes, — and he must
   die :
Much hath been done, but more remains to do —
Their galleys blaze — why not their city too?"

Quick at the word, — they seized him each a torch,
And fire the dome from minaret to porch.
A stern delight was fix'd in Conrad's eye,
But sudden sunk ; for on his ear the cry
Of women struck, and like the deadly knell
Knock'd at that heart unmoved by battle's yell.
" Oh ! burst the Haram — wrong not on your lives
One female form ; remember — *we* have wives.
On them such outrage Vengeance will repay ;
Man is our foe, and such 't is ours to slay ;
But still we spared — must spare the weaker prey
Oh ! I forgot — but Heaven will not forgive
If at my word the helpless cease to live :
Follow who will — I go — we yet have time
Our souls to lighten of at least a crime."
He climbs the crackling stair — he bursts the door,
Nor feels his feet grow scorching with the floor ;
His breath choked gasping with the volumed
   smoke,
But still from room to room his way he broke.
They search — they find — they save : with lusty
   arms

Each bears a prize of unregarded charms :
Calm their loud fears: sustain their sinking frames
With all the care defenceless beauty claims:
So well could Conrad tame their fiercest mood,
And check the very hands with gore imbued.
But who is she whom Conrad's arms convey
From reeking pile and combat's wreck away?
Who but the love of him he dooms to bleed?
The Haram queen — but still the slave of Seyd !

Brief time had Conrad now to greet Gulnare,*
Few words to reassure the trembling fair ;
For in that pause compassion snatch'd from war,
The foe before retiring, fast and far,
With wonder saw their footsteps unpursued,
First slowlier fled — then rallied — then withstood.
This Seyd perceives, then first perceives how few,
Compared with his, the Corsair's roving crew,
And blushes o'er his error, as he eyes
The ruin wrought by panic and surprise.
Alla il Alla ! Vengeance swells the cry —
Shame mounts to rage that must atone or die !
And flame for flame and blood for blood must tell,
The tide of triumph ebbs that flow'd too well —
When wrath returns to renovated strife,
And those who fought for conquest strike for life.

* Gulnare, a female name. It means, literally, the flower of the pomegranate.

Conrad beheld the danger — he beheld
His followers faint by freshening foes repell'd !
" One effort — one — to break the circling host ! "
They form — unite — charge — waver — all is lost !
Within a narrower ring compress'd, beset,
Hopeless, not heartless, strive and struggle yet —
Ah ! now they fight in firmest file no more,
Hemm'd in — cut off — cleft down — and trampled
    o'er;
But each strikes singly, silently, and home,
And sinks outwearied rather than o'ercome,
His last faint quittance rendering with his breath,
Till the blade glimmers in the grasp of death !

VII.

But first, ere came the rallying host to blows,
And rank to rank, and hand to hand oppose,
Gulnare and all her Haram handmaids freed,
Safe in the dome of one who held their creed,
By Conrad's mandate safely were bestow'd,
And dried those tears for life and fame that flow'd
And when that dark-eyed lady, young Gulnare,
Recall'd those thoughts late wandering in despair,
Much did she marvel o'er the courtesy
That smooth'd his accents; soften'd in his eye :
'T was strange — *that* robber thus with gore bedew'd
Seem'd gentler then than Seyd in fondest mood.
The Pacha woo'd as if he deem'd the slave
Must seem delighted with the heart he gave ;

The Corsair vow'd protection, soothed affright
As if his homage were a woman's right.
"The wish is wrong — nay, worse for female —
    vain :
Yet much I long to view that chief again ;
If but to thank for, what my fear forgot,
The life — my loving lord remember'd not !"

VIII.

And him she saw, where thickest carnage spread,
But gather'd breathing from the happier dead ;
Far from his band, and battling with a host
That deem right dearly won the field he lost,
Fell'd — bleeding — baffled of the death he sought,
And snatch'd to expiate all the ills he wrought ;
Preserved to linger and to live in vain,
While Vengeance ponder'd o'er new plans of pain,
And stanch'd the blood she saves to shed again —
But drop by drop, for Seyd's unglutted eye
Would doom him ever dying — ne'er to die !
Can this be he? triumphant late she saw,
When his red hand's wild gesture waved, a law
'T is he, indeed — disarm'd, but undeprest,
His sole regret the life he still possest ;
His wounds too slight, though taken with that will,
Which would have kiss'd the hand that then could
    kill.
Oh, were there none, of all the many given,
To send his soul — he scarcely ask'd to heaven !

Must he alone of all retain his breath,
Who more than all had striven and struck for death?
He deeply felt — what mortal hearts must feel,
When thus reversed on faithless Fortune's wheel,
For crimes committed, and the victor's threat
Of lingering tortures to repay the debt,
He deeply, darkly felt; but evil pride
That led to perpetrate — now nerves to hide.
Still in his stern and self-collected mien,
A conqueror's more than captive's air is seen,
Though faint with wasting toil and stiffening wound,
But few that saw — so calmly gazed around:
Though the far-shouting of the distant crowd,
Their tremors o'er, rose insolently loud,
The better warriors who beheld him near,
Insulted not the foe who taught them fear;
And the grim guards that to his durance led,
In silence eyed him with a secret dread.

IX

The Leech was sent — but not in mercy — there,
To note how much the life yet left could bear;
He found enough to load with heaviest chain,
And promise feeling for the wrench of pain:
To-morrow — yea — to-morrow's evening sun
Will sinking see impalement's pangs begun,
And rising with the wonted blush of morn

Behold how well or ill those pangs are borne.
Of torments this the longest and the worst,
Which adds all other agony to thirst,
That day by day death still forbears to slake,
While famish'd vultures flit around the stake.
"Oh! water — water!" — smiling Hate denies
The victim's prayer; for if he drinks, he dies.
This was his doom: the Leech, the guard, were
    gone,
And left proud Conrad fetter'd and alone.

X.

'T were vain to paint to what his feelings grew —
It even were doubtful if their victim knew
There is a war, a chaos of the mind,
When all its elements convulsed — combined —
Lie dark and jarring with perturbed force,
And gnashing with impenitent Remorse;
That juggling fiend — who never spake before —
But cries, "I warn'd thee!" when the deed is o'er.
Vain voice! the spirit burning but unbent,
May writhe — rebel — the weak alone repent!
Even in that lonely hour when most it feels,
And to itself, all — all that self reveals,
No single passion, and no ruling thought
That leaves the rest as once unseen, unsought;
But the wild prospect when the soul reviews, —
All rushing through their thousand avenues,
Ambition's dreams expiring, love's regret,

Endanger'd glory, life itself beset ;
The joy untasted, the contempt or hate
'Gainst those who fain would triumph in our fate ;
The hopeless past, the hasting future driven
Too quickly on to guess of hell or heaven ;
Deeds, thoughts, and words, perhaps remember'd
    not
So keenly till that hour, but ne'er forgot ;
Things light or lovely in their acted time,
But now to stern reflection each a crime ;
The withering sense of evil unreveal'd,
Not cankering less because the more conceal'd —
All, in a word, from which all eyes must start,
That open sepulchre — the naked heart,
Bares with its buried woes, till Pride awake,
To snatch the mirror from the soul — and break.
Ay, Pride can veil, and Courage brave it all,
All — all — before — beyond — the deadliest fall.
Each hath some fear, and he who least betrays,
The only hypocrite deserving praise :
Not the loud recreant wretch who boasts and flies ;
But he who looks on death — and silent dies.
So steel'd by pondering o'er his far career,
He half-way meets him should he menace near !

XI.

In the high chamber of his highest tower
Sate Conrad, fetter'd in the Pacha's power.
His palace perish'd in the flame — this fort

Contain'd at once his captive and his court.
Not much could Conrad of his sentence blame,
His foe, if vanquish'd, had but shared the same : —
Alone he sate — in solitude — had scann'd
His guilty bosom, but that breast he mann'd :
One thought alone he could not — dared not meet —
" Oh, how these tidings will Medora greet ? "
Then — only then — his clanking hands he raised,
And strain'd with rage the chain on which he gazed ;
But soon he found — or feign'd — or dream'd relief,
And smiled in self-derision of his grief.
" And now come torture when it will — or may,
More need of rest to nerve me for the day ! "
This said, with languor to his mat he crept,
And, whatso'er his visions, quickly slept.
'T was hardly midnight when that fray begun,
For Conrad's plans matured, at once were done :
And Havoc loathes so much the waste of time,
She scarce had left an uncommitted crime.
One hour beheld him since the tide he stemm'd —
Disguised, discover'd, — conquering, — ta'en, — condemn'd —
A chief on land, an outlaw on the deep —
Dēstroying, — saving, — prison'd, — and asleep !

He slept in calmest seeming, for his breath
Was hush'd so deep — Ah ! happy if in death !

He slept — Who o'er his placid slumber bends?
His foes are gone, and here he hath no friends;
Is it some seraph sent to grant him grace?
No, 't is an earthly form with heavenly face!
Its white arm raised a lamp — yet gently hid,
Lest the ray flash abruptly on the lid
Of that closed eye, which opens but to pain,
And once unclosed — but once may close again.
That form with eye so dark, and cheek so fair,
And auburn waves of gemm'd and braided hair;
With shape of fairy lightness — naked foot,
That shines like snow, and falls on earth as mute —
Through guards and dunnest night how came it
    there?
Ah! rather ask what will not woman dare?
Whom youth and pity lead like thee, Gulnare!
She could not sleep — and while the Pacha's rest
In muttering dreams yet saw his pirate-guest,
She left his side — his signet-ring she bore,
Which oft in sport adorn'd her hand before —
And with it, scarcely question'd, won her way
Through drowsy guards that must that sign obey.
Worn out with toil, and tired with changing blows,
Their eyes had envied Conrad his repose;
And chill and nodding at the turret door,
They stretch their listless limbs, and watch no
    more:
Just raised their heads to hail the signet-ring,
Nor ask or what or who the sign may bring.

She gazed in wonder: "Can he calmly sleep,
While other eyes his fall or ravage weep?
And mine in restlessness are wandering here —
What sudden spell hath made this man so dear?
True — 't is to him my life, and more, I owe,
And me and mine he spared from worse than woe:
'T is late to think — but soft — his slumber breaks —
How heavily he sighs! — he starts — awakes!"

He raised his head; — and dazzled with the light,
His eye seem'd dubious if it saw aright:
He moved his hand — the grating of his chain
Too harshly told him that he lived again.
"What is that form? if not a shape of air,
Methinks, my jailor's face shows wondrous fair!"

"Pirate! thou know'st me not; — but I am one,
Grateful for deeds thou hast too rarely done:
Look on me — and remember her thy hand
Snatch'd from the flames, and thy more fearful band.
I come through darkness, and I scarce know why —
Yet not to hurt — I would not see thee die."
"If so, kind lady! thine the only eye
That would not hear in that gay hope delight:
Theirs is the chance — and let them use their right

She gazed in wonder: " Can he
 calmly sleep,
While other eyes his fall or ravage
 weep?" . . .

But still I thank their courtesy or thine,
That would confess me at so fair a shrine!"

Strange though it seem, — yet with extremest grief
Is link'd a mirth — it doth not bring relief —
That playfulness of Sorrow ne'er beguiles,
And smiles in bitterness — but still it smiles;
And sometimes with the wisest and the best,
Till even the scaffold echoes with their jest!
Yet not the joy to which it seems akin —
It may deceive all hearts, save that within.
Whate'er it was that flash'd on Conrad, now
A laughing wildness half unbent his brow:
And these his accents had a sound of mirth,
As if the last he could enjoy on earth;
Yet 'gainst his nature — for through that short life,
Few thoughts had he to spare from gloom and strife

XIV.

" Corsair! thy doom is named — but I have power
To sooth the Pacha in his weaker hour
Thee would I spare — nay more — would save thee now,
But this — time — hope — nor even thy strength allow;
But all I can, I will: at least delay
The sentence that remits thee scarce a day.
More now were ruin — even thyself were loth
The vain attempt should bring but doom to both."

" Yes ! — loth indeed : — my soul is nerved to all,
Or fall'n too low to fear a further fall :
Tempt not thyself with peril; me with hope
Of flight from foes with whom I could not cope :
Unfit to vanquish — shall I meanly fly,
The one of all my band that would not die?
Yet there is one — to whom my memory clings,
Till to these eyes her own wild softness springs.
My sole resources in the path I trod
Were these — my bark, my sword, my love, my God.
The last I left in youth — He leaves me now —
And Man but works His will to lay me low.
I have no thought to mock His throne with prayer
Wrung from the coward crouching of despair;
It is enough — I breathe — and I can bear.
My sword is shaken from the worthless hand
That might have better kept so true a brand :
My bark is sunk or captive ; but my love —
For her in sooth my voice would mount above :
Oh ! she is all that still to earth can bind —
And this will break a heart so more than kind,
And blight a form — till thine appear'd, Gulnare,
Mine eye ne'er ask'd if others were so fair "

" Thou lov'st another then ? — but what to me
Is this ? — 't is nothing — nothing e'er can be :
But yet — thou lov'st — and — oh ! I envy those
Whose hearts on hearts as faithful can repose,
Who never feel the void — the wandering thought
That sighs o'er visions — such as mine hath
  wrought."

"Lady — methought thy love was his, for whom
This arm redeem'd thee from a fiery tomb."

"My love stern Seyd's! Oh — No — No — not
  my love:
Yet much this heart, that strives no
    strove
To meet his passion — but it would not be.
I felt — I feel — love dwells with — with the free.
I am a slave, a favour'd slave at best,
To share his splendour, and seem very blest!
Oft must my soul the question undergo,
Of — 'Dost thou love?' and burn to answer,
    'No!'
Oh! hard it is that fondness to sustain,
And struggle not to feel averse in vain;
But harder still the heart's recoil to bear,
And hide from one — perhaps another there.
He takes the hand I give not — nor withhold —
Its pulse nor check'd, nor quicken'd — calmly cold:
And when resign'd, it drops a lifeless weight
From one I never loved enough to hate.
No warmth these lips return by his imprest,
And chill'd remembrance shudders o'er the rest.
Yes — had I ever proved that passion's zeal,
The change to hatred were at least to feel:
But still he goes unmourn'd, returns unsought,
And oft when present — absent from my thought.
Or when reflection comes, and come it must —
I fear that henceforth 't will but bring disgust;

I am his slave — but, in despite of pride,
'T were worse than bondage to become his bride.
Oh! that this dotage of his breast would cease;
Or seek another and give mine release —
But yesterday — I could have said, to peace!
Yes — if unwonted fondness now I feign,
Remember — captive, 't is to break thy chain;
Repay the life that to thy hand I owe;
To give thee back to all endear'd below,
Who share such love as I can never know.
Farewell — morn breaks — and I must now away;
'T will cost me dear — but dread no death to-day!"

XV.

She press'd his fetter'd fingers to her heart,
And bow'd her head, and turn'd her to depart,
And noiseless as a lovely dream is gone.
And was she here? and is he now alone?
What gem hath dropp'd and sparkles o'er his chain?
The tear more sacred, shed for others' pain,
That starts at once — bright — pure — from Pity's mine,
Already polish'd by the hand divine!

Oh! too convincing — dangerously dear —
In woman's eye the unanswerable tear!
That weapon of her weakness she can wield,
To save, subdue — at once her spear and shield:
Avoid it — Virtue ebbs and Wisdom errs,

Too fondly gazing on that grief of hers!
What lost a world, and bade a hero fly?
The timid tear in Cleopatra's eye.
Yet be the soft triumvir's fault forgiven;
By this — how many lose not earth — but heaven!
Consign their souls to man's eternal foe,
And seal their own to spare some wanton's woe!

XVI.

'T is morn — and o'er his alter'd features play
The beams — without the hope of yesterday.
What shall he be ere night? perchance a thing
O'er which the raven flaps her funeral wing:
By his closed eye unheeded and unfelt,
While sets that sun, and dews of evening melt,
Chill, wet, and misty round each stiffened limb,
Refreshing earth — reviving all but him!

CANTO THE THIRD.

"Come vedi—ancor non m'abbandona." — DANTE.

I.

Slow sinks, more lovely ere his race be run,
Along Morea's hills the setting sun;
Not, as in northern climes, obscurely bright,
But one unclouded blaze of living light!
O'er the hush'd deep the yellow beam he throws,
Gilds the green wave, that trembles as it glows.
On old Ægina's rock, and Idra's isle,
The god of gladness sheds his parting smile;
O'er his own regions lingering, loves to shine,
Though there his altars are no more divine.
Descending fast, the mountain shadows kiss
Thy glorious gulf, unconquer'd Salamis!
Their azure arches through the long expanse

More deeply purpled meet his mellowing glance,
And tenderest tints, along their summits driven,
Mark his gay course, and own the hues of heaven;
Till, darkly shaded from the land and deep,
Behind his Delphian cliff he sinks to sleep.

On such an eve, his palest beam he cast,
When — Athens! here thy Wisest look'd his last.
How watch'd thy better sons his farewell ray,
That closed their murder'd sage's latest day!
Not yet — not yet — Sol pauses on the hill —
The precious hour of parting lingers still;
But sad his light to agonizing eyes,
And dark the mountain's once delightful dyes:
Gloom o'er the lovely land he seem'd to pour,
The land where Phœbus never frown'd before;
But e'er he sank below Cithæron's head,
The cup of woe was quaff'd — the spirit fled;
The soul of him who scorn'd to fear or fly —
Who lived and died, as none can live or die!
But lo! from high Hymettus to the plain,
The queen of night asserts her silent reign.
No murky vapour, herald of the storm,
Hides her fair face, nor girds her glowing form;
With cornice glimmering as the moonbeams play,
There the white column greets her grateful ray,
And, bright around with quivering beams beset,
Her emblem sparkles o'er the minaret:
The groves of olive scatter'd dark and wide
Where meek Cephisus pours his scanty tide,

The cypress saddening by the sacred mosque,
The gleaming turret of the gay kiosk,*
And, dun and sombre 'mid the holy calm,
Near Theseus' fane yon solitary palm,
All tinged with varied hues, arrest the eye —
And dull were his that pass'd them heedless by.

Again the Ægean, heard no more afar,
Lulls his chafed breast from elemental war;
Again his waves in milder tints unfold
Their long array of sapphire and of gold,
Mix'd with the shades of many a distant isle,
That frown — where gentler ocean seems to smile.

Not now my theme — why turn my thoughts to thee?
Oh! who can look along thy native sea,
Nor dwell upon thy name, whate'er the tale,
So much its magic must o'er all prevail?
Who that beheld that Sun upon thee set,
Fair Athens! could thine evening face forget?
Not he — whose heart nor time nor distance frees,
Spell-bound within the clustering Cyclades!
Nor seems this homage foreign to his strain,
His Corsair's isle was once thine own domain —
Would that with freedom it were thine again!

* The kiosk is a Turkish summer-house.

The Sun hath sunk — and, darker than the night,
Sinks with its beam upon the beacon height —
Medora's heart — the third day's come and
    gone —
With it he comes not — sends not — faithless one!
The wind was fair though light; and storms were
    none
Last eve Anselmo's bark return'd, and yet
His only tidings that they had not met!
Though wild, as now, far different were the tale
Had Conrad waited for that single sail.

The night-breeze freshens — she that day had
    pass'd
In watching all that Hope proclaim'd a mast;
Sadly she sate — on high — Impatience bore
At last her footsteps to the midnight shore;
And there she wander'd, heedless of the spray
That dash'd her garments oft, and warn'd away:
She saw not, felt not this — nor dared depart,
Nor deem'd it cold — her chill was at her heart;
Till grew such certainty from that suspense —
His very sight had shock'd from life or sense!

It came at last — a sad and shatter'd boat,
Whose inmates first beheld whom first they sought;
Some bleeding — all most wretched — these the
    few —

Scarce knew they how escaped — *this* all they
    knew.
In silence, darkling, each appear'd to wait
His fellow's mournful guess at Conrad's fate:
Something they would have said; but seem'd to
    fear
To trust their accents to Medora's ear.
She saw at once, yet sank not — trembled not —
Beneath that grief, that loneliness of lot,
Within that meek fair form, were feelings high,
That deem'd not, till they found their energy.
While yet was Hope, they soften'd, flutter'd,
    wept —
All lost — that softness died not — but it slept;
And o'er its slumber rose that Strength which said,
"With nothing left to love, there's nought to
    dread."
'T is more than nature's — like the burning might
Delirium gathers from the fever's height.

"Silent you stand — nor would I hear you tell
What — speak not — breathe not — for I know it
    well —
Yet would I ask — almost my lip denies
The — quick your answer — tell me where he lies."

"Lady! we know not — scarce with life we fled;
But here is one denies that he is dead:
He saw him bound; and bleeding — but alive."

She heard no further — 't was in vain to strive —
So throbb'd each vein — each thought — till then
    withstood;
Her own dark soul — these words at once subdued:
She totters — falls — and senseless had the wave
Perchance but snatch'd her from another grave:
But that with hands though rude, yet weeping eyes,
They yield such aid as Pity's haste supplies:
Dash o'er her death-like cheek the ocean dew,
Raise — fan — sustain — till life returns anew;
Awake her handmaids, with the matrons leave
That fainting form o'er which they gaze and grieve;
Then seek Anselmo's cavern, to report
The tale too tedious — when the triumph short.

In that wild council, words wax'd warm and
    strange,
With thoughts of ransom, rescue, and revenge;
All, save repose or flight : still lingering there
Breathed Conrad's spirit, and forbade despair ;
Whate'er his fate — the breasts he form'd and led,
Will save him living, or appease him dead.
Woe to his foes! there yet survive a few,
Whose deeds are daring as their hearts are true.

Within the Haram's secret chamber sate
Stern Seyd, still pondering o'er his Captive's fate;

His thoughts on love and hate alternate dwell,
Now with Gulnare, and now in Conrad's cell;
Here at his feet the lovely slave reclined
Surveys his brow — would soothe his gloom of mind:
While many an anxious glance her large dark eye
Sends in its idle search for sympathy,
His only bends in seeming o'er his beads,*
But inly views his victim as he bleeds.
" Pacha! the day is thine ; and on thy crest
Sits Triumph — Conrad taken — fall'n the rest !
His doom is fix'd — he dies : and well his fate
Was earn'd — yet much too worthless for thy hate :
Methinks, a short release, for ransom told
With all his treasure, not unwisely sold:
Report speaks largely of his pirate-hoard —
Would that of this my Pacha were the lord !
While baffled, weaken'd by this fatal fray —
Watch'd — follow'd — he were then an easier prey ;
But once cut off — the remnant of his band
Embark their wealth, and seek a safer strand."

"Gulnare ! — if for each drop of blood a gem
Were offer'd rich as Stamboul's diadem ;
If for each hair of his a massy mine
Of virgin ore should supplicating shine;
If all our Arab tales divulge or dream

* The Comboloio, or Mahometan rosary.

Here at his feet the lovely slave
 reclined,
Surveys his brow — would soothe
 his gloom of mind.

Of wealth were here — that gold should not
    redeem!
It had not now redeem'd a single hour,
But that I know him fetter'd, in my power;
And, thirsting for revenge, I ponder still
On pangs that longest rack, and latest kill."
"Nay, Seyd! — I seek not to restrain thy rage,
Too justly moved for mercy to assuage;
My thoughts were only to secure for thee
His riches — thus released, he were not free;
Disabled, shorn of half his might and band,
His capture could but wait thy first command."

"His capture *could!* — and shall I then resign
One day to him — the wretch already mine?
Release my foe! — at whose remonstrance? —
    thine!
Fair suitor! — to thy virtuous gratitude,
That thus repays this Giaour's relenting mood,
Which thee and thine alone of all could spare,
No doubt — regardless if the prize were fair,
My thanks and praise alike are due — now hear!
I have a counsel for thy gentler ear:
I do mistrust thee, woman! and each word
Of thine stamps truth on all Suspicion heard.
Borne in his arms through fire from yon Serai —
Say, wert thou lingering there with him to fly?
Thou need'st not answer — thy confession speaks,
Already reddening on thy guilty cheeks;

Then, lovely dame, bethink thee, and beware!
'T is not *his* life alone may claim such care!
Another word and — nay — I need no more.
Accursed was the moment when he bore
Thee from the flames, which better far — but
    no —
I then had mourn'd thee with a lover's woe —
Now, 't is thy lord that warns — deceitful thing!
Know'st thou that I can clip thy wanton wing?
In words alone I am not wont to chafe:
Look to thyself — nor deem thy falsehood safe!"

He rose — and slowly, sternly thence withdrew,
Rage in his eye and threats in his adieu:
Ah! little reck'd that chief of womanhood —
Which frowns ne'er quell'd, nor menaces subdued;
And little deem'd he what thy heart, Gulnare,
When soft could feel, and when incensed could
    dare.
His doubts appear'd to wrong — nor yet she knew
How deep the root from whence compassion
    grew —
She was a slave — from such may captives claim
A fellow-feeling, differing but in name;
Still half-unconscious — heedless of his wrath,
Again she ventured on the dangerous path,
Again his rage repell'd — until arose
That strife of thought, the source of woman's
    woes!

Meanwhile — long, anxious — weary, still — the same
Roll'd day and night — his soul could terror tame —
This fearful interval of doubt and dread,
When every hour might doom him worse than dead,
When every step that echo'd by the gate
Might entering lead where axe and stake await;
When every voice that grated on his ear
Might be the last that he could ever hear;
Could terror tame — that spirit stern and high
Had proved unwilling as unfit to die;
'T was worn — perhaps decay'd — yet silent bore
That conflict deadlier far than all before:
The heat of fight, the hurry of the gale,
Leave scarce one thought inert enough to quail;
But bound and fix'd in fetter'd solitude,
To pine, the prey of every changing mood;
To gaze on thine own heart; and meditate
Irrevocable faults, and coming fate —
Too late the last to shun — the first to mend —
To count the hours that struggle to thine end,
With not a friend to animate, and tell
To other ears that death became thee well;
Around thee foes to forge the ready lie,
And blot life's latest scene with calumny;

Before thee tortures, which the soul can dare,
Yet doubts how well the shrinking flesh may bear;
But deeply feels a single cry would shame,
To valour's praise thy last and dearest claim;
The life thou leav'st below, denied above
By kind monopolists of heavenly love;
And more than doubtful paradise — thy heaven
Of earthly hope — thy loved one from thee riven.
Such were the thoughts that outlaw must sustain,
And govern pangs surpassing mortal pain:
And those sustain'd he — boots it well or ill?
Since not to sink beneath, is something still!

VII.

The first day pass'd — he saw not her — Gulnare —
The second — third — and still she came not there;
But what her words avouch'd, her charms had done,
Or else he had not seen another sun.
The fourth day roll'd along, and with the night
Came storm and darkness in their mingling might:
Oh! how he listen'd to the rushing deep,
That ne'er till now so broke upon his sleep;
And his wild spirit wilder wishes sent,
Roused by the roar of his own element!
Oft had he ridden on that winged wave,
And loved its roughness for the speed it gave;
And now its dashing echo'd on his ear,
A long known voice — alas, too vainly near!

Loud sung the wind above ; and, doubly loud,
Shook o'er his turret cell the thunder-cloud ;
And flash'd the lightning by the latticed bar,
To him more genial than the midnight star :
Close to the glimmering grate he dragg'd his chain,
And hoped *that* peril might not prove in vain.
He raised his iron hand to Heaven, and pray'd
One pitying flash to mar the form it made :
His steel and impious prayer attract alike —
The storm roll'd onward, and disdain'd to strike ;
Its peal wax'd fainter — ceased — he felt alone,
As if some faithless friend had spurn'd his groan.

The midnight pass'd, and to the massy door
A light step came — it paused — it moved once more ;
Slow turns the grating bolt and sullen key :
'T is as his heart foreboded — that fair she !
Whate'er her sins, to him a guardian saint,
And beauteous still as hermit's hope can paint :
Yet changed since last within that cell she came,
More pale her cheek, more tremulous her frame :
On him she cast her dark and hurried eye,
Which spoke before her accents — "Thou must die !
Yes, thou must die — there is but one resource,
The last — the worst — if torture were not worse."

"Lady! I look to none — my lips proclaim
What last proclaim'd they — Conrad still the same:
Why should'st thou seek an outlaw's life to spare,
And change the sentence I deserve to bear?
Well have I earn'd — nor here alone — the meed
Of Seyd's revenge, by many a lawless deed."

"Why should I seek? because — oh, didst thou not
Redeem my life from worse than slavery's lot?
Why should I seek? — hath misery made thee blind
To the fond workings of a woman's mind?
And must I say? albeit my heart rebel
With all that woman feels, but should not tell —
Because — despite thy crimes — that heart moved:
It fear'd thee — thank'd thee — pitied — madden'd
    — loved.
Reply not, tell not now thy tale again,
Thou lov'st another — and I love in vain;
Though fond as mine her bosom, form more fair,
I rush through peril which she would not dare.
If that thy heart to hers were truly dear,
Were I thine own — thou wert not lonely here:
An outlaw's spouse — and leave her lord to roam!
What hath such gentle dame to do with home?
But speak not now — o'er thine and o'er my head
Hangs the keen sabre by a single thread;

THE CORSAIR.

If thou hast courage still, and would'st be free,
Receive this poniard — rise — and follow me!"

"Ay, in my chains! my steps will gently tread,
With these adornments, o'er each slumbering head!
Thou hast forgot — is this a garb for flight?
Or is that instrument more fit for fight?"

" Misdoubting Corsair I have gain'd the guard,
Ripe for revolt, and greedy for reward.
A single word of mine removes that chain:
Without some aid how here could I remain?
Well, since we met, hath sped my busy time,
If in aught evil, for thy sake the crime:
The crime — 't is none to punish those of Seyd.
That hated tyrant, Conrad — he must bleed!
I see thee shudder — but my soul is changed —
Wrong'd — spurn'd — reviled — and it shall be aveng'd —
Accused of what till now my heart disdain'd —
Too faithful, though to bitter bondage chain'd.
Yes, smile! — but he had little cause to sneer,
I was not treacherous then — nor thou too dear:
But he has said it — and the jealous well,
Those tyrants, teasing, tempting to rebel,
Deserve the fate their fretting lips foretell.
I never loved — he bought me — somewhat high —
Since with me came a heart he could not buy.
I was a slave unmurmuring; he hath said,

But for his rescue I with thee had fled.
'T was false thou know'st — but let such augurs rue,
Their words are omens Insult renders true.
Nor was thy respite granted to my prayer ;
This fleeting grace was only to prepare
New torments for thy life, and my despair.
Mine too he threatens ; but his dotage still
Would fain reserve me for his lordly will :
When wearier of these fleeting charms and me,
There yawns the sack — and yonder rolls the sea !
What, am I then a toy for dotard's play,
To wear but till the gilding frets away ?
I saw thee — loved thee — owe thee all — would save,
If but to show how grateful is a slave.
But had he not thus menaced fame and life
(And well he keeps his oaths pronounced in strife),
I still had saved thee — but the Pacha spared.
Now I am all thine own — for all prepared ·
Thou lov'st me not — nor know'st — or but the worst.
Alas! this love — that hatred are the first —
Oh! couldst thou prove my truth, thou wouldst not start,
Nor fear the fire that lights an Eastern heart ;
'T is now the beacon of thy safety — now
It points within the port a Mainote prow :
But in one chamber, where our path must lead
There sleeps — he must not wake — the oppressor Seyd !"

"Gulnare — Gulnare — I never felt till now
My abject fortune, wither'd fame so low :
Seyd is mine enemy; had swept my band
From earth with ruthless but with open hand ;
And therefore came I, in my bark of war,
To smite the smiter with the scimitar ;
Such is my weapon — not the secret knife —
Who spares a woman's seeks not slumber's life.
Thine saved I gladly, Lady, not for this —
Let me not deem that mercy shown amiss.
Now fare thee well — more peace be with thy
    breast !
Night wears apace — my last of earthly rest ! "

"Rest ! rest ! by sunrise must thy sinews shake,
And thy limbs writhe around the ready stake.
I heard the order — saw — I will not see —
If thou wilt perish, I will fall with thee.
My life, my love, my hatred — all below
Are on this cast — Corsair ! 't is but a blow!
Without it flight were idle — how evade
His sure pursuit ? my wrongs too unrepaid,
My youth disgraced — the long, long wasted years,
One blow shall cancel with our future fears ;
But since the dagger suits thee less than brand,
I 'll try the firmness of a female hand.
The guards are gain'd — one moment all were
    o'er —
Corsair ! we meet in safety or no more ;

If errs my feeble hand, the morning cloud
Will hover o'er thy scaffold, and my shroud."

She turn'd, and vanish'd ere he could reply,
But his glance follow'd far with eager eye ;
And gathering, as he could, the links that bound
His form, to curl their length, and curb their sound,
Since bar and bolt no more his steps preclude,
He, fast as fetter'd limbs allow, pursued.
'T was dark and winding, and he knew not where
That passage led ; nor lamp nor guard was there :
He sees a dusky glimmering — shall he seek
Or shun that ray so indistinct and weak ?
Chance guides his steps — a freshness seems to bear
Full on his brow, as if from morning air ;
He reach'd an open gallery — on his eye
Gleam'd the last star of night, the clearing sky :
Yet scarcely heeded these — another light
From a lone chamber struck upon his sight.
Towards it he moved ; a scarcely closing door
Reveal'd the ray within, but nothing more.
With hasty step a figure outward pass'd,
Then paused — and turn'd — and paused — 't is She at last !
No poniard in that hand, nor sign of ill —

"Thanks to that softening heart, she could not
    kill!"
Again he look'd, the wildness of her eye
Starts from the day abrupt and fearfully.
She stopp'd — threw back her dark far-floating
    hair,
That nearly veil'd her face and bosom fair;
As if she late had bent her leaning head
Above some object of her doubt or dread.
They meet — upon her brow — unknown — forgot —
Her hurrying hand had left — 't was but a spot —
Its hue was all he saw, and scarce withstood —
Oh! slight but certain pledge of crime — 't is blood!

x.

He had seen battle — he had brooded lone
O'er promised pangs to sentenced guilt foreshown;
He had been tempted, — chasten'd, — and the
    chain
Yet on his arms might ever there remain;
But ne'er from strife, captivity, remorse —
From all his feelings in their inmost force —
So thrill'd, so shudder'd every creeping vein,
As now they froze before that purple stain.
That spot of blood, that light but guilty streak,
Had banish'd all the beauty from her cheek!
Blood he had view'd — could view unmoved — but
    then
It flow'd in combat, or was shed by men!

XI.

" 'T is done — he nearly waked — but it is done.
Corsair! he perish'd — thou art dearly won.
All words would now be vain — away — away!
Our bark is tossing — 't is already day.
The few gain'd over, now are wholly mine,
And these thy yet surviving band shall join;
Anon my voice shall vindicate my hand,
When once our sail forsakes this hated strand."

XII.

She clapp'd her hands — and through the gallery pour,
Equipp'd for flight, her vassals — Greek and Moor;
Silent but quick they stoop, his chains unbind;
Once more his limbs are free as mountain wind!
But on his heavy heart such sadness sate,
As if they there transferr'd that iron weight.
No words are utter'd — at her sign, a door
Reveals the secret passage to the shore;
The city lies behind — they speed, they reach
The glad waves dancing on the yellow beach;
And Conrad following, at her beck, obey'd,
Nor cared he now if rescued or betray'd;
Resistance were as useless as if Seyd
Yet lived to view the doom his ire decreed.

XIII.

Embark'd, the sail unfurl'd, the light breeze blew —
How much had Conrad's memory to review!

Sunk he in Contemplation, till the cape
Where last he anchor'd rear'd its giant shape.
Ah ! since that fatal night, though brief the time,
Had swept an age of terror, grief, and crime.
As its far shadow frown'd above the mast,
He veil'd his face ; and sorrow'd as he pass'd :
He thought of all — Gonsalvo and his band,
His fleeting triumph and his failing hand ;
He thought on her afar, his lonely bride :
He turn'd and saw — Gulnare, the homicide !

XIV.

She watch'd his features till she could not bear
Their freezing aspect and averted air,
And that strange fierceness foreign to her eye,
Fell quench'd in tears, too late to shed or dry.
She knelt beside him, and his hand she press'd,
" Thou may'st forgive though Allah's self detest ;
But for that deed of darkness, what wert thou ?
Reproach me — but not yet — O ! spare me *now* !
I am not what I seem — this fearful night
My brain bewildered — do not madden quite !
If I had never loved — though less my guilt,
Thou hadst not lived to — hate me — if thou wilt."

XV.

She wrongs his thoughts, they more himself upbraid
Than her, though undesign'd, the wretch he made :

But speechless all, deep, dark, and unexprest,
They bleed within that silent cell — his breast.
Still onward, fair the breeze, nor rough the surge,
The blue waves sport around the stern they urge ;
Far on the horizon's verge appears a speck,
A spot — a mast — a sail — an armed deck !
Their little bark her men of watch descry,
And ampler canvas woos the wind from high ;
She bears her down majestically near,
Speed on her prow, and terror in her tier :
A flash is seen — the ball beyond their bow
Booms harmless, hissing to the deep below.
Up rose keen Conrad from his silent trance,
A long, long absent gladness in his glance : —
"'T is mine — my blood-red flag! again — again —
I am not all deserted on the main !"
They own the signal, answer to the hail,
Hoist out the boat at once, and slacken sail.
" 'T is Conrad! Conrad !" shouting from the deck,
Command nor duty could their transport check !
With light alacrity and gaze of pride,
They view him mount once more his vessel's side ;
A smile relaxing in each rugged face,
Their arms can scarce forbear a rough embrace.
He, half forgetting danger and defeat,
Returns their greeting as a chief may greet,
Wrings with a cordial grasp Anselmo's hand,
And feels he yet can conquer and command !

XVI.

These greetings o'er, the feelings that o'erflow,
Yet grieve to win him back without a blow;
They sail'd prepared for vengeance — had they known
A woman's hand secured that deed her own,
She were their queen — less scrupulous are they
Than haughty Conrad how they win their way.
With many an asking smile, and wondering stare,
They whisper round, and gaze upon Gulnare;
And her, at once above — beneath her sex,
Whom blood appall'd not, their regards perplex.
To Conrad turns her faint imploring eye,
She drops her veil, and stands in silence by;
Her arms are meekly folded on that breast,
Which — Conrad safe — to fate resign'd the rest.
Though worse than frenzy could that bosom fill,
Extreme in love or hate, in good or ill,
The worst of crimes had left her woman still.

XVII.

This Conrad mark'd, and felt — ah! could he less?
Hate of that deed — but grief for her distress;
What she has done no tears can wash away,
And Heaven must punish on its angry day:
But — it was done: he knew, whate'er her guilt,
For him that poniard smote, that blood was spilt;
And he was free! — and she for him had given

Her all on earth, and more than all in heaven!
And now he turn'd him to that dark-eyed slave,
Whose brow was bow'd beneath the glance he gave,
Who now seem'd changed and humbled, faint and meek,
But varying oft the colour of her cheek
To deeper shades of paleness — all its red
That fearful spot which stain'd it from the dead!
He took that hand — it trembled — now too late —
So soft in love, so wildly nerved in hate;
He clasp'd that hand — it trembled — and his own
Had lost its firmness, and his voice its tone.
"Gulnare!" — but she replied not — "dear Gulnare!"
She raised her eye — her only answer there —
At once she sought and sunk in his embrace:
If he had driven her from that resting-place,
His had been more or less than mortal heart,
But — good or ill — it bade her not depart.
Perchance, but for the bodings of his breast,
His latest virtue then had join'd the rest.
Yet even Medora might forgive the kiss
That ask'd from form so fair no more than this,
The first, the last that Frailty stole from Faith —
To lips where Love had lavish'd all his breath,
To lips — whose broken sighs such fragrance fling,
As he had fann'd them freshly with his wing!

XVIII.

They gain by twilight's hour their lonely isle.
To them the very rocks appear to smile;
The haven hums with many a cheering sound,
The beacons blaze their wonted stations round,
The boats are darting o'er the curly bay,
And sportive dolphins bend them through the spray;
Even the hoarse sea-bird's shrill, discordant shriek,
Greets like the welcome of his tuneless beak!
Beneath each lamp that through its lattice gleams,
Their fancy paints the friends that trim the beams.
Oh! what can sanctify the joys of home,
Like Hope's gay glance from Ocean's troubled foam!

XIX.

The lights are high on beacon and from bower,
And 'midst them Conrad seeks Medora's tower:
He looks in vain — 't is strange — and all remark,
Amid so many, hers alone is dark.
'T is strange — of yore its welcome never fail'd,
Nor now perchance extinguish'd, only veil'd.
With the first boat descends he for the shore,
And looks impatient on the lingering oar.
Oh! for a wing beyond the falcon's flight,
To bear him like an arrow to that height?
With the first pause the resting rowers gave,
He waits not, looks not — leaps into the wave,

Strives through the surge, bestrides the beach, and high
Ascends the path familiar to his eye.
He reach'd his turret door — he paused — no sound
Broke from within; and all was night around.
He knock'd, and loudly — footstep nor reply
Announced that any heard or deem'd him nigh;
He knock'd, but faintly— for his trembling hand
Refused to aid his heavy heart's demand.
The portal opens — 't is a well-known face —
But not the form he panted to embrace.
Its lips are silent — twice his own essay'd,
And fail'd to frame the question they delayed;
He snatch'd the lamp — its light will answer all —
It quits his grasp, expiring in the fall.
He would not wait for that reviving ray —
As soon could he have linger'd there for day;
But, glimmering through the dusky corridore,
Another chequers o'er the shadow'd floor;
His steps the chamber gain — his eyes behold
All that his heart believed not — yet foretold!

XX.

He turn'd not — spoke not — sunk not — fix'd his look,
And set the anxious frame that lately shook:
He gazed — how long we gaze despite of pain,
And know, but dare not own, we gaze in vain!

In life itself she was so still and fair,
That death with gentler aspect wither'd there :
And the cold flowers her colder hand contain'd,
In that last grasp as tenderly were strain'd
As if she scarcely felt, but feign'd a sleep,
And made it almost mockery yet to weep.
The long dark lashes fringed her lids of snow,
And veil'd — thought shrinks from all that lurk'd
    below —
Oh! o'er the eye death most exerts his might,
And hurls the spirit from her throne of light!
Sinks those blue orbs in that long last eclipse,
But spares, as yet, the charm around her lips —
Yet, yet they seem as they forbore to smile,
And wish'd repose — but only for a while ;
But the white shroud, and each extended tress,
Long — fair — but spread in utter lifelessness,
Which, late the sport of every summer wind,
Escaped the baffled wreath that strove to bind ;
These — and the pale pure cheek, became the bier —
But she is nothing — wherefore is he here ?

XXI.

He ask'd no question — all were answer'd now
By the first glance on that still, marble brow.
It was enough — she died — what reck'd it how ?
The love of youth, the hope of better years,
The source of softest wishes, tenderest fears,
The only living thing he could not hate,

Was reft at once — and he deserved his fate,
But did not feel it less: — the good explore,
For peace, those realms where guilt can never soar;
The proud, the wayward, who have fix'd below
Their joy, and find this earth enough for woe,
Lose in that one their all — perchance a mite —
But who in patience parts with all delight?
Full many a stoic eye and aspect stern
Mask hearts where grief hath little left to learn:
And many a withering thought lies hid, not lost,
In smiles that least befit who wear them most.

XXII.

By those, that deepest feel, is ill exprest
The indistinctness of the suffering breast;
Where thousand thoughts begin to end in one,
Which seeks from all the refuge found in none;
No words suffice the secret soul to show,
And Truth denies all eloquence to Woe.
On Conrad's stricken soul exhaustion prest,
And stupor almost lull'd it into rest:
So feeble now — his mother's softness crept
To those wild eyes, which like an infant's wept:
It was the very weakness of his brain,
Which thus confess'd without relieving pain.
None saw his trickling tears — perchance, if seen,
That useless flood of grief had never been:
Nor long they flow'd — he dried them to depart,
In helpless — hopeless — brokenness of heart:

The sun goes forth — but Conrad's day is dim;
And the night cometh — ne'er to pass from him.
There is no darkness like the cloud of mind,
On Grief's vain eye — the blindest of the blind!
Which may not — dare not see — but turns aside
To blackest shade — nor will endure a guide!

XXIII.

His heart was form'd for softness — warp'd to wrong;
Betray'd too early, and beguiled too long;
Each feeling pure — as falls the dropping dew
Within the grot; like that had harden'd too;
Less clear, perchance, its earthly trials pass'd,
But sunk, and chill'd, and petrified at last.
Yet tempests wear, and lightning cleaves the rock;
If such his heart, so shatter'd it the shock.
There grew one flower beneath its rugged brow,
Though dark the shade — it shelter'd — saved till now.
The thunder came — that bolt hath blasted both,
The Granite's firmness and the Lily's growth:
The gentle plant hath left no leaf to tell
Its tale, but shrunk and wither'd where it fell;
And of its cold protector, blacken round
But shiver'd fragments on the barren ground!

XXIV.

'T is morn — to venture on his lonely hour
Few dare; though now Anselmo sought his tower.

He was not there — nor seen along the shore;
Ere night, alarm'd, their isle is traversed o'er:
Another morn — another bids them seek,
And shout his name till echo waxeth weak :
Mount, grotto, cavern, valley search'd in vain,
They find on shore a sea-boat's broken chain ;
Their hope revives — they follow o'er the main.
'Tis idle all — moons roll on moons away,
And Conrad comes not—came not since that day :
Nor trace, nor tidings of his doom declare
Where lives his grief, or perish'd his despair !
Long mourn'd his band whom none could mourn
 beside ;
And fair the monument they gave his bride :
For him they raise not the recording stone —
His death yet dubious, deeds too widely known ;
He left a Corsair's name to other times,
Link'd with one virtue, and a thousand crimes.

LARA.

LARA.

CANTO THE FIRST.

I.

THE Serfs are glad through Lara's wide domain,*
And slavery half forgets her feudal chain ;
He, their unhoped, but unforgotten lord,
The long self-exiled chieftain, is restored :
There be bright faces in the busy hall,
Bowls on the board, and banners on the wall ;

* The reader is apprised that the name of Lara being Spanish, and no circumstance of local or national description fixing the scene or hero of the poem to any country or age, the word "Serf" which could not be correctly applied to the lower classes in Spain, who were never vassals of the soil, has nevertheless been employed to designate the followers of our fictitious chieftain. He is meant for noble of the Morea.

Far chequering o'er the pictured window, plays
The unwonted fagots' hospitable blaze;
And gay retainers gather round the hearth,
With tongues all loudness, and with eyes all mirth.

The chief of Lara is return'd again:
And why had Lara cross'd the bounding main?
Left by his sire, too young such loss to know,
Lord of himself;—that heritage of woe,
That fearful empire which the human breast
But holds to rob the heart within of rest!—
With none to check, and few to point in time
The thousand paths that slope the way to crime;
Then, when he most required commandment, then
Had Lara's daring boyhood govern'd men.
It skills not, boots not, step by step to trace
His youth through all the mazes of its race;
Short was the course his restlessness had run,
But long enough to leave him half undone.

III.

And Lara left in youth his fatherland;
But from the hour he waved his parting hand
Each trace wax'd fainter of his course, till all
Had nearly ceased his memory to recall.
His sire was dust, his vassals could declare,
'T was all they knew, that Lara was not there;
Nor sent, nor came he, till conjecture grew

Cold in the many, anxious in the few.
His hall scarce echoes with his wonted name,
His portrait darkens in its fading frame.
Another chief consoled his destined bride,
The young forgot him, and the old had died;
" Yet doth he live!" exclaims the impatient heir,
And sighs for sables which he must not wear.
A hundred scutcheons deck with gloomy grace
The Lara's last and longest dwelling-place;
But one is absent from the mouldering file,
That now were welcome in that Gothic pile.

IV

He comes at last in sudden loneliness,
And whence they know not, why they need not
    guess;
They more might marvel, when the greeting's o'er,
Not that he came, but came not long before:
No train is his beyond a single page,
Of foreign aspect, and of tender age.
Years had roll'd on, and fast they speed away
To those that wander as to those that stay;
But lack of tidings from another clime
Had lent a flagging wing to weary Time.
They see, they recognize, yet almost deem
The present dubious, or the past a dream.

He lives, nor yet is past his manhood's prime,
Though sear'd by toil, and something touch'd by
    time;

His faults, whate'er they were, if scarce forgot,
Might be untaught him by his varied lot;
Nor good nor ill of late were known, his name
Might yet uphold his patrimonial fame.
His soul in youth was haughty, but his sins
No more than pleasure from the stripling wins;
And such, if not yet harden'd in their course,
Might be redeem'd, nor ask a long remorse.

V.

And they indeed were changed — 't is quickly seen,
Whate'er he be, 't was not what he had been:
That brow in furrow'd lines had fix'd at last,
And spake of passions, but of passion past;
The pride, but not the fire, of early days,
Coldness of mien, and carelessness of praise;
A high demeanour, and a glance that took
Their thoughts from others by a single look;
And that sarcastic levity of tongue,
The stinging of a heart the world hath stung,
That darts in seeming playfulness around,
And makes those feel that will not own the wound:
All these seem'd his, and something more beneath
Than glance could well reveal, or accent breathe.
Ambition, glory, love, the common aim,
That some can conquer, and that all would claim,
Within his breast appear'd no more to strive,
Yet seem'd as lately they had been alive;
And some deep feeling it were vain to trace
At moments lighten'd o'er his livid face.

Not much he loved long question of the past,
Nor told of wondrous wilds, and deserts vast,
In those far lands where he had wander'd lone,
And — as himself would have it seem — unknown:
Yet these in vain his eye could scarcely scan,
Nor glean experience from his fellow-man;
But what he had beheld he shunn'd to show,
As hardly worth a stranger's care to know;
If still more prying such inquiry grew,
His brow fell darker, and his words more few.

Not unrejoiced to see him once again,
Warm was his welcome to the haunts of men;
Born of high lineage, link'd in high command,
He mingled with the Magnates of his land;
Join'd the carousals of the great and gay,
And saw them smile or sigh their hours away;
But still he only saw, and did not share
The common pleasure or the general care:
He did not follow what they all pursued,
With hope still baffled, still to be renew'd;
Nor shadowy honour, nor substantial gain,
Nor beauty's preference, and the rival's pain:
Around him some mysterious circle thrown
Repell'd approach, and show'd him still alone;
Upon his eye sate something of reproof,

That kept at least frivolity aloof;
And things more timid that beheld him near,
In silence gazed, or whisper'd mutual fear;
And they the wiser, friendlier few confess'd
They deem'd him better than his air express'd.

VIII.

'T was strange — in youth all action and all life,
Burning for pleasure, not averse from strife;
Woman — the field — the ocean — all that gave
Promise of gladness, peril of a grave,
In turn he tried — he ransack'd all below,
And found his recompense in joy or woe,
No tame, trite medium; for his feelings sought
In that intenseness an escape from thought:
The tempest of his heart in scorn had gazed
On that the feebler elements had raised:
The rapture of his heart had look'd on high,
And ask'd if greater dwelt beyond the sky:
Chain'd to excess, the slave of each extreme,
How woke he from the wildness of that dream?
Alas! he told not; — but he did awake
To curse the wither'd heart that would not break.

IX.

Books, for his volume heretofore was Man,
With eye more curious he appear'd to scan;
And oft, in sudden mood, for many a day
From all communion he would start away:

And then, his rarely call'd attendants said,
Through night's long hours would sound his hurried
    tread
O'er the dark gallery, where his fathers frown'd
In rude but antique portraiture around.
They heard, but whisper'd — "*that* must not be
    known —
The sound of words less earthly than his own.
Yes, they who chose might smile, but some had seen
They scarce knew what, but more than should have
    been.
Why gazed he so upon the ghastly head
Which hands profane had gather'd from the dead,
That still beside his open'd volume lay,
As if to startle all save him away?
Why slept he not when others were at rest?
Why heard no music, and received no guest?
All was not well, they deem'd; but where the
    wrong?
Some knew perchance — but 't were a tale too long;
And such besides were too discreetly wise,
To more than hint their knowledge in surmise;
But if they would — they could" — around the
    board,
Thus Lara's vassals prattled of their lord.

x.

It was the night — and Lara's glassy stream
The stars are studding, each with imaged beam:

So calm, the waters scarcely seem to stray,
And yet they glide like happiness away;
Reflecting far and fairy-like from high
The immortal lights that live along the sky:
Its banks are fringed with many a goodly tree,
And flowers the fairest that may feast the bee:
Such in her chaplet infant Dian wove,
And Innocence would offer to her love.
These deck the shore; the waves their channel make
In windings bright and mazy like the snake.
All was so still, so soft in earth and air,
You scarce would start to meet a spirit there;
Secure that nought of evil could delight
To walk in such a scene, on such a night!
It was a moment only for the good:
So Lara deem'd, nor longer there he stood,
But turn'd in silence to his castle-gate;
Such scene his soul no more could contemplate:
Such scene reminded him of other days,
Of skies more cloudless, moons of purer blaze,
Of nights more soft and frequent, hearts that now —
No — no — the storm may beat upon his brow,
Unfelt — unsparing; but a night like this,
A night of beauty, mock'd such breast as his.

XI.

He turn'd within his solitary hall,
And his high shadow shot along the wall:
There were the painted forms of other times,

'T was all they left of virtues or of crimes,
Save vague traditions; and the gloomy vaults
That hid their dust, their foibles, and their faults;
And half a column of the pompous page,
That speeds the specious tale from age to age,
Where history's pen its praise or blame supplies,
And lies like truth, and still most truly lies.
He wandering mused, and as the moonbeam shone
Through the dim lattice o'er the floor of stone,
And the high fretted roof, and saints, that there
O'er Gothic windows knelt in picture prayer,
Reflected in fantastic figures grew,
Like life, but not like mortal life, to view;
His bristling locks of sable, brow of gloom,
And the wide waving of his shaken plume,
Glanced like a spectre's attributes, and gave
His aspect all that terror gives the grave.

XII.

'T was midnight — all was slumber; the lone light
Dimm'd in the lamp, as loth to break the night.
Hark! there be murmurs heard in Lara's hall —
A sound — a voice — a shriek — a fearful call!
A long, loud shriek — and silence — did they hear
That frantic echo burst the sleeping ear?
They heard and rose, and tremulously brave
Rush where the sound invoked their aid to save:
They come with half-lit tapers in their hands,
And snatch'd in startled haste unbelted brands.

XIII.

Cold as the marble where his length was laid,
Pale as the beam that o'er his features play'd,
Was Lara stretch'd; his half-drawn sabre near,
Dropp'd it should seem in more than nature's fear;
Yet he was firm, or had been firm till now,
And still defiance knit his gather'd brow;
Though mix'd with terror, senseless as he lay,
There lived upon his lip the wish to slay;
Some half-form'd threat in utterance there had died,
Some imprecation of despairing pride:
His eye was almost seal'd, but not forsook
Even in its trance the gladiator's look,
That oft awake his aspect could disclose,
And now was fix'd in horrible repose.
They raise him — bear him: hush! he breathes, he speaks,
The swarthy blush recolours in his cheeks,
His lip resumes its red; his eye, though dim,
Rolls wide and wild, each slowly quivering limb
Recalls its function, but his words are strung
In terms that seem not of his native tongue;
Distinct but strange, enough they understand
To deem them accents of another land:
And such they were, and meant to meet an ear
That hears him not — alas, that cannot hear!

Glanced like a spectre's attributes,
　　　　　　　　　and gave
His aspect all that terror gives the
　　　　　　　grave. . . .

XIV.

His page approach'd, and he alone appear'd
To know the import of the words they heard;
And by the changes of his cheek and brow,
They were not such as Lara should avow,
Nor he interpret, yet with less surprise
Than those around their chieftain's state he eyes,
But Lara's prostrate form he bent beside,
And in that tongue which seem'd his own replied,
And Lara heeds those tones that gently seem
To soothe away the horrors of his dream;
If dream it were, that thus could overthrow
A breast that needed not ideal woe.

XV.

Whate'er his frenzy dream'd or eye beheld,
If yet remember'd ne'er to be reveal'd,
Rests at his heart: the custom'd morning came,
And breathed new vigour in his shaken frame;
And solace sought he none from priest nor leech,
And soon the same in movement and in speech
As heretofore he fill'd the passing hours,
Nor less he smiles, nor more his forehead lowers
Than these were wont; and if the coming night
Appear'd less welcome now to Lara's sight,
He to his marvelling vassals show'd it not,
Whose shuddering proved *their* fear was less forgot.
In trembling pairs (alone they dared not) crawl
The astonish'd slaves, and shun the fated hall;

The waving banner, and the clapping door;
The rustling tapestry, and the echoing floor,
The long dim shadows of surrounding trees,
The flapping bat, the night-song of the breeze;
Aught they behold or hear their thought appals,
As evening saddens o'er the dark grey walls.

XVI.

Vain thought! that hour of ne'er unravell'd gloom
Came not again, or Lara could assume
A seeming of forgetfulness, that made
His vassals more amazed, nor less afraid.
Had memory vanish'd then with sense restored?
Since word, nor look, nor gesture of their lord
Betray'd a feeling that recall'd to these
That fever'd moment of his mind's disease.
Was it a dream? was his the voice that spoke
Those strange wild accents? his the cry that broke
Their slumber? his the oppress'd o'er-labour'd heart
That ceased to beat, the look that made them start?
Could he who thus had suffer'd, so forget,
When such as saw that suffering shudder yet?
Or did that silence prove his memory fix'd
Too deep for words, indelible, unmix'd
In that corroding secrecy which gnaws
The heart to show the effect, but not the cause?
Not so in him; his breast had buried both,
Nor common gazers could discern the growth

Of thoughts that mortal lips must leave half told ;
They choke the feeble words that would unfold.

XVII.

In him inexplicably mix'd appear'd
Much to be loved and hated, sought and fear'd ;
Opinion varying o'er his hidden lot,
In praise or railing ne'er his name forgot :
His silence form'd a theme for others' prate —
They guess'd — they gazed — they fain would know
    his fate.
What had he been ? what was he, thus unknown,
Who walk'd their world, his lineage only known?
A hater of his kind? yet some would say,
With them he could seem gay amidst the gay ;
But own'd that smile, if oft observed and near,
Waned in its mirth, and wither'd to a sneer ;
That smile might reach his lip, but pass'd not by,
None e'er could trace its laughter to his eye :
Yet there was softness too in his regard,
At times, a heart as not by nature hard,
But once perceived, his spirit seem'd to chide
Such weakness, as unworthy of its pride,
And steel'd itself, as scorning to redeem
One doubt from others' half withheld esteem ;
In self-inflicted penance of a breast
Which tenderness might once have wrung from rest ,
In vigilance of grief, that would compel
The soul to hate for having loved too well.

XVIII.

There was in him a vital scorn of all;
As if the worst had fall'n which could befall,
He stood a stranger in this breathing world,
An erring spirit from another hurled;
A thing of dark imaginings, that shaped
By choice the perils he by chance escaped;
But 'scaped in vain, for in their memory yet
His mind would half exult and half regret:
With more capacity for love than earth
Bestows on most of mortal mould and birth,
His early dreams of good outstripp'd the truth,
And troubled manhood follow'd baffled youth;
With thought of years in phantom chase misspent,
And wasted powers for better purpose lent:
And fiery passions that had pour'd their wrath
In hurried desolation o'er his path,
And left the better feelings all at strife
In wild reflection o'er his stormy life;
But haughty still, and loth himself to blame,
He call'd on Nature's self to share the shame,
And charged all faults upon the fleshly form
She gave to clog the soul, and feast the worm;
Till he at last confounded good and ill,
And half mistook for fate the acts of will:
Too high for common selfishness, he could
At times resign his own for others' good,
But not in pity, not because he ought,
But in some strange perversity of thought,

That sway'd him onward with a secret pride
To do what few or none would do beside;
And this same impulse would, in tempting time,
Mislead his spirit equally to crime;
So much he soar'd beyond, or sunk beneath
The men with whom he felt condemn'd to breathe,
And longed by good or ill to separate
Himself from all who shared his mortal state;
His mind abhorring, this had fix'd her throne
Far from the world, in regions of her own;
Thus coldly passing all that pass'd below,
His blood in temperate seeming now would flow:
Ah! happier if it ne'er with guilt had glow'd,
But ever in that icy smoothness flow'd.
'T is true, with other men their path he walk'd,
And like the rest in seeming did and talk'd;
Nor outraged Reason's rules by flaw nor start,
His madness was not of the head, but heart;
And rarely wandered in his speech, or drew
His thoughts so forth as to offend the view.

XIX.

With all that chilling mystery of mien,
And seeming gladness to remain unseen;
He had (if 't were not nature's boon) an art
Of fixing memory on another's heart:
It was not perchance love, — nor hate — nor aught
That words can image to express the thought;
But they who saw him did not see in vain,

And once beheld, would ask of him again :
And those to whom he spake remember'd well,
And on the words, however light, would dwell :
None knew nor how, nor why, but he entwined
Himself perforce around the hearer's mind :
There he was stamp'd, in liking, or in hate,
If greeted once ; however brief the date
That friendship, pity, or aversion knew,
Still there within the inmost thought he grew.
You could not penetrate his soul, but found,
Despite your wonder, to your own he wound :
His presence haunted still ; and from the breast
He forced an all-unwilling interest.
Vain was the struggle in that mental net,
His spirit seem'd to dare you to forget !

XX.

There is a festival, where knights and dames,
And aught that wealth or lofty lineage claims,
Appear — a high-born and a welcomed guest
To Otho's hall came Lara with the rest.
The long carousal shakes the illumined hall,
Well speeds alike the banquet and the ball;
And the gay dance of bounding Beauty's train
Links grace and harmony in happiest chain ;
Blest are the early hearts and gentle hands
That mingle there in well-according bands.
It is a sight the careful brow might smooth,
And make age smile, and dream itself to youth,

And Youth forget such hour was pass'd on earth,
So springs the exulting bosom to that mirth!

XXI.

And Lara gazed on these, sedately glad;
His brow belied him if his soul was sad;
And his glance follow'd fast each fluttering fair,
Whose steps of lightness woke no echo there.
He lean'd against the lofty pillar nigh,
With folded arms and long attentive eye,
Nor mark'd a glance so sternly fix'd on his:
Ill brook'd high Lara scrutiny like this.
At length he caught it, 't is a face unknown,
But seems as searching his, and his alone;
Prying and dark, a stranger's by his mien,
Who still till now had gazed on him unseen;
At length encountering meets the mutual gaze
Of keen inquiry, and of mute amaze:
On Lara's glance emotion gathering grew,
As if distrusting that the stranger threw;
Along the stranger's aspect fix'd and stern
Flash'd more than thence the vulgar eye could learn.

XXII.

"'T is he!" the stranger cried, and those that heard,
Re-echo'd fast and far the whisper'd word.
"'T is he!"—"'T is who?" they question far and near,

Till louder accents rung on Lara's ear;
So widely spread, few bosoms well could brook
The general marvel, or that single look.
But Lara stirr'd not, changed not : the surprise
That sprung at first to his arrested eyes
Seem'd now subsided : neither sunk nor raised
Glanced his eye round, though still the stranger
    gazed ;
And drawing nigh, exclaim'd, with haughty sneer,
" 'T is he ! — how came he thence ? — what doth he
    here ? "

XXIII.

It were too much for Lara to pass by
Such questions, so repeated fierce and high :
With look collected, but with accent cold,
More mildly firm than petulantly bold,
He turn'd, and met the inquisitorial tone —
" My name is Lara ! — when thine own is known,
Doubt not my fitting answer to requite
The unlook'd-for courtesy of such a knight.
'T is Lara ! — further wouldst thou mark or ask ?
I shun no question, and I wear no mask."

" Thou shunn'st no question ? Ponder — is there
    none
Thy heart must answer, though thine ear would
    shun ?
And deem'st thou me unknown too ? Gaze again!
At least thy memory was not given in vain.

Oh! never canst thou cancel half her debt,
Eternity forbids thee to forget."
With slow and searching glance upon his face
Grew Lara's eyes, but nothing there could trace.
They knew, or chose to know : with dubious look
He deign'd no answer, but his head he shook,
And half contemptuous turn'd to pass away;
But the stern stranger motion'd him to stay.
" A word ! — I charge thee stay, and answer here
To one who, wert thou noble, were thy peer;
But as thou wast and art — nay, frown not, lord,
If false, 't is easy to disprove the word —
But as thou wast and art, on thee looks down,
Distrusts thy smiles, but shakes not at thy frown.
Art thou not he, whose deeds — "
                              " Whate'er I be,
Words wild as these, accusers like to thee,
I list no further; those with whom they weigh
May hear the rest, nor venture to gainsay
The wondrous tale no doubt thy tongue can tell,
Which thus begins so courteously and well.
Let Otho cherish here his polish'd guest,
To him my thanks and thoughts shall be express'd."
And here their wondering host hath interposed :
" Whate'er there be between you undisclosed,
This is no time nor fitting place to mar
The mirthful meeting with a wordy war.
If thou, Sir Ezzelin, hast aught to show

Which it befits Count Lara's ear to know,
To-morrow, here, or elsewhere as may best
Beseem your mutual judgment, speak the rest;
I pledge myself for thee, as not unknown,
Though like Count Lara now return'd alone
From other lands, almost a stranger grown;
And if from Lara's blood and gentle birth
I augur right of courage and of worth,
He will not that untainted line belie,
Nor aught that knighthood may accord, deny."

"To-morrow be it," Ezzelin replied,
"And here our several worth and truth be tried;
I gage my life, my falchion, to attest
My words; so may I mingle with the blest!"
What answers Lara? to its centre shrunk
His soul, in deep abstraction sudden sunk.
The words of many, and the eyes of all
That there were gather'd, seem'd on him to fall;
But his were silent, his appear'd to stray
In far forgetfulness away — away —
Alas! that heedlessness of all around
Bespoke remembrance only too profound.

XXIV.

"To-morrow!—ay, to-morrow!" Further word
Than those repeated none from Lara heard.
Upon his brow no outward passion spoke,
From his large eye no flashing anger broke;

Yet there was something fix'd in that low tone
Which show'd resolve, determined, though unknown.
He seized his cloak — his head he slightly bow'd,
And passing Ezzelin he left the crowd:
And, as he pass'd him, smiling met the frown
With which that chieftain's brow would bear him down.
It was nor smile of mirth, nor struggling pride
That curbs to scorn the wrath it cannot hide;
But that of one in his own heart secure
Of all that he would do, or could endure.
Could this mean peace? the calmness of the good?
Or guilt grown old in desperate hardihood?
Alas! too like in confidence are each
For man to trust to mortal look or speech;
From deeds, and deeds alone, may he discern
Truths which it wrings the unpractised heart to learn.

XXV.

And Lara called his page, and went his way —
Well could that stripling word or sign obey:
His only follower from those climes afar
Where the soul glows beneath a brighter star;
For Lara left the shore from whence he sprung,
In duty patient, and sedate though young;
Silent as him he served, his fate appears
Above his station, and beyond his years.

Though not unknown the tongue of Lara's land,
In such from him he rarely heard command;
But fleet his step, and clear his tones would come,
When Lara's lip breathed forth the words of home.
Those accents, as his native mountains dear,
Awake their absent echoes in his ear;
Friends', kindreds', parents', wonted voice recall,
Now lost, abjured, for one — his friend, his all :
For him earth now disclosed no other guide ;
What marvel, then, he rarely left his side?

XXVI.

Light was his form, and darkly delicate
That brow whereon his native sun had sate,
But had not marr'd, though in his beams he grew,
The cheek where oft the unbidden blush shone through;
Yet not such blush as mounts when health would show
All the heart's hue in that delighted glow ;
But 't was a hectic tint of secret care
That for a burning moment fever'd there.
And the wild sparkle of his eye seem'd caught
From high, and lighten'd with electric thought,
Though its black orb those long low lashes' fringe
Had temper'd with a melancholy tinge ;
Yet less of sorrow than of pride was there,
Or, if 't were grief, a grief that none should share :

And pleased not him the sports that please his age,
The tricks of youth, the frolics of the page.
For hours on Lara he would fix his glance,
As all-forgotten in that watchful trance;
And from his chief withdrawn, he wander'd lone,
Brief were his answers, and his questions none:
His walk the wood, his sport some foreign book :
His resting-place the bank that curbs the brook :
He seem'd like him he served, to live apart
From all that lures the eye, and fills the heart;
To know no brotherhood, and take from earth
No gift beyond that bitter boon — our birth.

XXVII.

If aught he loved, 't was Lara: but was shown
His faith in reverence and in deeds alone;
In mute attention ; and his care, which guess'd
Each wish, fulfill'd it ere the tongue express'd.
Still there was haughtiness in all he did,
A spirit deep that brook'd not to be chid :
His zeal, though more than that of servile hands,
In act alone obeys, his air commands:
As if 't was Lara's less than *his* desire
That thus he served, but surely not for hire.
Slight were the tasks enjoin'd him by his lord,
To hold the stirrup, or to bear the sword ;
To tune his lute, or, if he will'd it more,
On tomes of other times and tongues to pore;
But ne'er to mingle with the menial train,

To whom he show'd nor deference nor disdain,
But that well-worn reserve which proved he knew
No sympathy with that familiar crew;
His soul, whate'er his station or his stem,
Could bow to Lara, not descend to them.
Of higher birth he seem'd, and better days;
Nor mark of vulgar toil that hand betrays,
So femininely white, it might bespeak
Another sex, when matched with that smooth cheek,
But for his garb, and something in his gaze,
More wild and high than woman's eye betrays;
A latent fierceness that far more became
His fiery climate than his tender frame:
True, in his words it broke not from his breast,
But from his aspect might be more than guess'd.
Kaled his name, though rumour said he bore
Another ere he left his mountain shore;
For sometimes he would hear, however nigh,
That name repeated loud without reply,
As unfamiliar; or, if roused again,
Start to the sound, as but remember'd then;
Unless 't was Lara's wonted voice that spake,
For then, ear, eyes, and heart would all awake.

XXVIII.

He had look'd down upon the festive hall,
And mark'd that sudden strife so mark'd of all;
And when the crowd around and near him told

Their wonder at the calmness of the bold,
Their marvel how the high-born Lara bore
Such insult from a stranger, doubly sore,
The colour of young Kaled went and came,
The lip of ashes, and the cheek of flame;
And o'er his brow the dampening heart-drops threw
The sickening iciness of that cold dew,
That rises as the busy bosom sinks
With heavy thoughts from which reflection shrinks.
Yes, there be things which we must dream and dare,
And execute before thought be half aware;
Whate'er might Kaled's be, it was enow
To seal his lip, but agonize his brow.
He gazed on Ezzelin till Lara cast
That sidelong smile upon the knight he pass'd;
When Kaled saw that smile his visage fell,
As if on something recognized right well:
His memory read in such a meaning more
Than Lara's aspect unto others wore,
Forward he sprung — a moment, both were gone,
And all within that hall seem'd left alone;
Each had so fix'd his eye on Lara's mien,
All had so mix'd their feelings with that scene,
That when his long dark shadow through the porch
No more relieves the glare of yon high torch,
Each pulse beats quicker, and all bosoms seem

To bound as doubting from too black a dream,
Such as we know is false, yet dread in sooth,
Because the worst is ever nearest truth.
And they are gone — but Ezzelin is there,
With thoughtful visage and imperious air ;
But long remain'd not: ere an hour expired
He waved his hand to Otho, and retired

XXIX.

The crowd are gone, the revellers at rest :
The courteous host, and all-approving guest,
Again to that accustom'd couch must creep
Where joy subsides, and sorrow sighs to sleep,
And man, o'erlabour'd with his being's strife,
Shrinks to that sweet forgetfulness of life :
There lie love's feverish hope, and cunning's guile,
Hate's working brain, and lull'd ambition's wile :
O'er each vain eye oblivion's pinions wave,
And quenched existence crouches in a grave.
What better name may slumber's bed become?
Night's sepulchre, the universal home,
Where weakness, strength, vice, virtue, sunk supine
Alike in naked helplessness recline ;
Glad for a while to heave unconscious breath,
Yet wake to wrestle with the dread of death,
And shun, though day but dawn on ills increased,
That sleep, the loveliest, since it dreams the least

CANTO THE SECOND.

NIGHT wanes — the vapours round the mountains curl'd
Melt into morn, and Light awakes the world
Man has another day to swell the past,
And lead him near to little, but his last;
But mighty Nature bounds as from her birth,
The sun is in the heavens, and life on earth;
Flowers in the valley, splendour in the beam,
Health on the gale, and freshness in the stream.
Immortal man! behold her glories shine,
And cry exulting inly, "They are thine!"
Gaze on, while yet thy gladden'd eye may see,
A morrow comes when they are not for thee;
And grieve what may above thy senseless bier,
Nor earth nor sky will yield a single tear;

Nor cloud shall gather more, nor leaf shall fall,
Nor gale breathe forth one sigh for thee, for all ;
But creeping things shall revel in their spoil,
And fit thy clay to fertilize the soil.

'T is morn — 't is noon — assembled in the hall,
The gather'd chieftains come to Otho's call :
'T is now the promised hour, that must proclaim
The life or death of Lara's future fame :
When Ezzelin his charge may here unfold,
And whatsoe'er the tale, it must be told.
His faith was pledged, and Lara's promise given,
To meet it in the eye of man and Heaven.
Why comes he not? Such truths to be divulged,
Methinks the accuser's rest is long indulged.

III.

The hour is past, and Lara too is there,
With self-confiding, coldly patient air ;
Why comes not Ezzelin? The hour is past,
And murmurs rise, and Otho's brows o'ercast.
" I know my friend! his faith I cannot fear,
If yet he be on earth, expect him here ;
The roof that held him in the valley stands
Between my own and noble Lara's lands ;
My halls from such a guest had honour gain'd,
Nor had Sir Ezzelin his host disdain'd,
But that some previous proof forbade his stay,

And urged him to prepare against to-day.
The word I pledged for his I pledge again,
Or will myself redeem his knighthood's stain."

He ceased; and Lara answer'd, "I am here
To lend at thy demand a listening ear,
To tales of evil from a stranger's tongue,
Whose words already might my heart have wrung,
But that I deem'd him scarcely less than mad,
Or, at the worst, a foe ignobly bad.
I know him not: but me it seems he knew
In lands where — but I must not trifle too:
Produce this babbler — or redeem the pledge:
Here in thy hold, and with thy falchion's edge."

Proud Otho on the instant, reddening, threw
His glove on earth, and forth his sabre flew.
"The last alternative befits me best,
And thus I answer for mine absent guest."

With cheek unchanging from its sallow gloom,
However near his own or other's tomb;
With hand, whose almost careless coolness spoke
Its grasp well used to deal the sabre-stroke;
With eye, though calm, determined not to spare,
Did Lara too his willing weapon bear.
In vain the circling chieftains round them closed,
For Otho's frenzy would not be opposed;
And from his lip those words of insult fell —
His sword is good who can maintain them well.

IV.

Short was the conflict; furious, blindly rash,
Vain Otho gave his bosom to the gash;
He bled, and fell; but not with deadly wound,
Stretch'd by a dexterous sleight along the ground.
"Demand thy life!" He answer'd not: and then
From that red floor he ne'er had risen again,
For Lara's brow upon the moment grew
Almost to blackness in its demon hue;
And fiercer shook his angry falchion now
Than when his foe's was levell'd at his brow.
Then all was stern collectedness and art,
Now rose the unleaven'd hatred of his heart;
So little sparing to the foe he fell'd,
That when the approaching crowd his arm withheld,
He almost turn'd the thirsty point on those
Who thus for mercy dared to interpose;
But to a moment's thought that purpose bent;
Yet look'd he on him still with eye intent,
As if he loathed the ineffectual strife
That left a foe, howe'er o'erthrown, with life;
As if to search how far the wound he gave
Had sent its victim onward to his grave.

V.

They raised the bleeding Otho, and the Leech
Forbade all present question, sign, and speech;
The others met within a neighbouring hall,
And he, incensed and heedless of them all,

The cause and conqueror in this sudden fray,
In haughty silence slowly strode away:
He back'd his steed, his homeward path he took,
Nor cast on Otho's towers a single look.

VI.

But where was he — that meteor of a night,
Who menaced but to disappear with light?
Where was this Ezzelin? who came and went
To leave no other trace of his intent.
He left the dome of Otho long ere morn,
In darkness; yet so well the path was worn,
He could not miss it: near his dwelling lay;
But there he was not, and with coming day
Came fast inquiry, which unfolded nought
Except the absence of the chief it sought.
A chamber tenantless, a steed at rest,
His host alarm'd, his murmuring squires distress'd.
Their search extends along, around the path,
In dread to meet the marks of prowler's wrath:
But none are there, and not a brake hath borne
Nor gout of blood, nor shred of mantle torn:
Nor fall nor struggle hath defaced the grass,
Which still retains a mark where murder was;
Nor dabbling fingers left to tell the tale,
The bitter print of each convulsive nail,
When agonized hands that ceased to guard,
Wound in that pang the smoothness of the sward
Some such had been, if here a life was reft,

But these were not; and doubting hope is left;
And strange suspicion, whispering Lara's name,
Now daily mutters o'er his blacken'd fame:
Then sudden silent when his form appear'd,
Awaits the absence of the thing it fear'd;
Again its wonted wondering to renew,
And dye conjecture with a darker hue.

VII.

Days roll along, and Otho's wounds are heal'd,
But not his pride; and hate no more conceal'd:
He was a man of power, and Lara's foe,
The friend of all who sought to work him woe:
And from his country's justice now demands
Account of Ezzelin at Lara's hands.
Who else than Lara could have cause to fear
His presence? who had made him disappear,
If not the man on whom his menaced charge
Had sate too deeply were he left at large?
The general rumour ignorantly loud,
The mystery dearest to the curious crowd;
The seeming friendlessness of him who strove
To win no confidence, and wake no love;
The sweeping fierceness which his soul betray'd,
The skill with which he wielded his keen blade;
Where had his arm unwarlike caught that art?
Where had that fierceness grown upon his heart?
For it was not the blind capricious rage
A word can kindle and a word assuage:

But the deep working of a soul unmix'd
With aught of pity where its wrath had fix'd :
Such as long power and overgorged success
Concentrates into all that 's merciless :
These, link'd with that desire which ever sways
Mankind, the rather to condemn than praise,
'Gainst Lara gathering raised at length a storm,
Such as himself might fear, and foes would form,
And he must answer for the absent head
Of one that haunts him still, alive or dead.

VIII.

Within that land was many a malcontent,
Who cursed the tyranny to which he bent ;
That soil full many a wringing despot saw,
Who work'd his wantonness in form of law.
Long war without and frequent broil within
Had made a path for blood and giant sin,
That waited but a signal to begin
New havoc, such as civil discord blends,
Which knows no neuter, owns but foes or friends :
Fix'd in his feudal fortress, each was lord,
In word and deed obey'd, in soul abhorr'd.
Thus Lara had inherited his lands,
And with them pining hearts and sluggish hands ;
But that long absence from his native clime
Had left him stainless of oppression's crime,
And now diverted by his milder sway,
All dread by slow degrees had worn away

The menials felt their usual awe alone,
But more for him than them that fear was grown.
They deem'd him now unhappy, though at first
Their evil judgment augur'd of the worst;
And each long restless night, and silent mood,
Was traced to sickness, fed by solitude:
And though his lonely habits threw of late
Gloom o'er his chamber, cheerful was his gate;
For thence the wretched ne'er unsoothed withdrew;
For them, at least, his soul compassion knew.
Cold to the great, contemptuous to the high,
The humble pass'd not his unheeding eye;
Much he would speak not, but beneath his roof
They found asylum oft, and ne'er reproof.
And they who watch'd might mark that, day by day,
Some new retainers gather'd to his sway;
But most of late, since Ezzelin was lost,
He play'd the courteous lord and bounteous host:
Perchance his strife with Otho made him dread
Some snare prepared for his obnoxious head;
Whate'er his view, his favour more obtains
With these, the people, than his fellow-thanes.
If this were policy, so far 't was sound,
The million judged but of him as they found;
From him by sterner chiefs to exile driven,
They but required a shelter, and 't was given.
By him no peasant mourn'd his rifled cot,
And scarce the serf could murmur o'er his lot;

With him old avarice found its hoard secure,
With him contempt forbore to mock the poor;
Youth present cheer and promised recompense
Detain'd, till all too late to part from thence:
To hate he offer'd, with the coming change,
The deep reversion of delay'd revenge:
To love, long baffled by the unequal match,
The well-won charms success was sure to snatch.
All now was rife, he waits but to proclaim
That slavery nothing which was still a name.
The moment came, the hour when Otho thought
Secure at last the vengeance which he sought;
His summons found the destined criminal
Begirt by thousands in his swarming hall,
Fresh from their feudal fetters newly riven,
Defying earth, and confident of heaven.
That morning he had freed the soil-bound slaves
Who dig no land for tyrants but their graves!
Such is their cry — some watchword for the fight
Must vindicate the wrong, and warp the right:
Religion — freedom — vengeance — what you will,
A word's enough to raise mankind to kill;
Some factious phrase by cunning caught and spread
That guilt may reign, and wolves and worms be
    fed.

IX.

Throughout that clime the feudal chiefs had gain'd
Such sway, their infant monarch hardly reign'd:

Now was the hour for faction's rebel growth,
The serfs contemn'd the one, and hated both:
They waited but a leader, and they found
One to their cause inseparably bound;
By circumstance compell'd to plunge again,
In self-defence, amidst the strife of men.
Cut off by some mysterious fate from those
Whom birth and nature meant not for his foes,
Had Lara from that night, to him accurst,
Prepared to meet, but not alone, the worst:
Some reason urged, whate'er it was, to shun
Inquiry into deeds at distance done;
By mingling with his own the cause of all,
E'en if he fail'd, he still delay'd his fall.
The sullen calm that long his bosom kept,
The storm that once had spent itself and slept,
Roused by events that seem'd foredoom'd to urge
His gloomy fortunes to their utmost verge,
Burst forth, and made him all he once had been,
And is again: he only changed the scene.
Light care had he for life, and less for fame,
But not less fitted for the desperate game:
He deem'd himself mark'd out for others' hate,
And mock'd at ruin, so they shared his fate.
What cared he for the freedom of the crowd?
He raised the humble but to bend the proud.
He had hoped quiet in his sullen lair,
But man and destiny beset him there:
Inured to hunters, he was found at bay,

And they must kill, they cannot snare the prey.
Stern, unambitious, silent, he had been
Henceforth a calm spectator of life's scene ;
But dragg'd again upon the arena, stood
A leader not unequal to the feud ;
In voice, mien, gesture, savage nature spoke,
And from his eye the gladiator broke.

What boots the oft-repeated tale of strife,
The feast of vultures, and the waste of life?
The varying fortune of each separate field,
The fierce that vanquish, and the faint that yield?
The smoking ruin, and the crumbled wall?
In this the struggle was the same with all ;
Save that distemper'd passions lent their force
In bitterness that banished all remorse.
None sued, for mercy knew her cry was vain,
The captive died upon the battle-plain ;
In either cause, one rage alone possess'd
The empire of the alternate victor's breast ;
And they that smote for freedom or for sway,
Deem'd few were slain while more remain to slay.
It was too late to check the wasting brand,
And Desolation reap'd the famish'd land ;
The torch was lighted, and the flame was spread,
And Carnage smiled upon her daily dead.

XI.

Fresh with the nerve the new-born impulse strung,
The first success to Lara's numbers clung:
But that vain victory hath ruin'd all;
They form no longer to their leader's call:
In blind confusion on the foe they press,
And think to snatch is to secure success.
The lust of beauty, and the thirst of hate,
Lure on the broken brigands to their fate:
In vain he doth whate'er a chief may do,
To check the headlong fury of that crew;
In vain their stubborn ardour he would tame,
The hand that kindles cannot quench the flame:
The wary foe alone hath turned their mood,
And shown their rashness to that erring brood:
The feign'd retreat, the nightly ambuscade,
The daily harass, and the fight delay'd,
The long privation of the hoped supply,
The tentless rest beneath the humid sky,
The stubborn wall that mocks the leaguer's art,
And palls the patience of his baffled heart,
Of these they had not deem'd: the battle-day
They could encounter as a veteran may;
But more preferr'd the fury of the strife,
And present death to hourly suffering life:
And famine wrings, and fever sweeps away
His numbers melting fast from their array;
Intemperate triumph fades to discontent,

And Lara's soul alone seems still unbent:
But few remain to aid his voice and hand,
And thousands dwindled to a scanty band:
Desperate, though few, the last and best remain'd
To mourn the discipline they late disdain'd.
One hope survives, the frontier is not far,
And thence they may escape from native war,
And bear within them to the neighbouring state
An exile's sorrows, or an outlaw's hate:
Hard is the task their fatherland to quit,
But harder still to perish or submit.

XII.

It is resolved — they march — consenting Night
Guides with her star their dim and torchless flight:
Already they perceive its tranquil beam
Sleep on the surface of the barrier stream;
Already they descry — is yon the bank?
Away! 't is lined with many a hostile rank.
Return or fly! — What glitters in the rear?
'T is Otho's banner — the pursuer's spear!
Are those the shepherds' fires upon the height?
Alas! they blaze too widely for the flight:
Cut off from hope, and compass'd in the toil,
Less blood, perchance, hath bought a richer spoil!

XIII.

A moment's pause, 't is but to breathe their band,
Or shall they onward press, or here withstand?

It matters little : — if they charge the foes
Who by the border-stream their march oppose,
Some few perchance may break and pass the line,
However link'd to baffle such design.
" The charge be ours ! to wait for their assault
Were fate well worthy of a coward's halt."
Forth flies each sabre, rein'd is every steed,
And the next word shall scarce outstrip the deed :
In the next tone of Lara's gathering breath,
How many shall but hear the voice of death!

XIV.

His blade is bared, in him there is an air
As deep, but far too tranquil for despair ;
A something of indifference more than then
Becomes the bravest, if they feel for men.
He turn'd his eye on Kaled, ever near,
And still too faithful to betray one fear ;
Perchance 't was but the moon's dim twilight threw
Along his aspect an unwonted hue
Of mournful paleness, whose deep tint express'd
The truth, and not the terror of his breast.
This Lara mark'd, and laid his hand on his ;
It trembled not in such an hour as this.
His lip was silent, scarcely beat his heart ;
His eye alone proclaim'd, " We will not part !
Thy band may perish, or thy friends may flee ;
Farewell to life, but not adieu to thee ! "

The word hath pass'd his lips, and onward driven,
Pours the link'd band through ranks asunder riven
Well has each steed obey'd the arm'd heel,
And flash the scimitars, and rings the steel.
Outnumber'd, not outbraved, they still oppose
Despair to daring, and a front to foes;
And blood is mingled with the dashing stream,
Which runs all redly till the morning beam.

XV.

Commanding, aiding, animating all,
Where foe appear'd to press, or friend to fall,
Cheers Lara's voice, and waves or strikes his steel,
Inspiring hope himself had ceased to feel.
None fled, for well they knew that flight were vain;
But those that waver turn to smite again,
While yet they find the firmest of the foe
Recoil before their leader's look and blow.
Now girt with numbers, now almost alone,
He foils their ranks, or reunites his own;
Himself he spared not — once they seem'd to fly —
Now was the time, he waved his hand on high,
And shook — Why sudden droops that plumed crest?
The shaft is sped — the arrow's in his breast!
That fatal gesture left the unguarded side,
And Death had stricken down yon arm of pride.
The word of triumph fainted from his tongue;
That hand, so raised, how droopingly it hung!

Why sudden droops that plumed crest?
The shaft is sped — the arrow's
in his breast. . . .

But yet the sword instinctively retains,
Though from its fellow shrink the falling reins.
These Kalad snatches; dizzy with the blow,
And senseless bending o'er his saddle-bow,
Perceives not Lara that his anxious page
Beguiles his charger from the combat's rage :
Meantime his followers charge, and charge again ;
Too mix'd the slayers now to heed the slain !

XVI.

Day glimmers on the dying and the dead,
The cloven cuirass, and the helmless head ;
The war-horse masterless is on the earth,
And that last gasp hath burst his bloody girth ;
And near, yet quivering with what life remain'd,
The heel that urged him, and the hand that rein'd.
And some too near that rolling torrent lie,
Whose waters mock the lip of those that die :
That panting thirst which scorches in the breath
Of those that die the soldier's fiery death,
In vain impels the burning mouth to crave
One drop — the last — to cool it for the grave ;
With feeble and convulsive effort swept
Their limbs along the crimson'd turf have crept ;
The faint remains of life such struggles waste,
But yet they reach the stream, and bend to taste :
They feel its freshness, and almost partake —
Why pause? — No further thirst have they to slake :
It is unquench'd, and yet they feel it not ;
It was an agony, — but now forgot !

XVII.

Beneath a lime, remoter from the scene,
Where but for him that strife had never been,
A breathing but devoted warrior lay :
'T was Lara bleeding fast from life away.
His follower once, and now his only guide,
Kneels Kaled watchful o'er his welling side,
And with his scarf would stanch the tides that rush
With each convulsion in a blacker gush ;
And then, as his faint breathing waxes low,
In feebler, not less fatal tricklings flow ;
He scarce can speak, but motions him 't is vain,
And merely adds another throb to pain.
He clasps the hand that pang which would assuage,
And sadly smiles his thanks to that dark page,
Who nothing fears, nor feels, nor heeds, nor sees,
Save that damp brow which rests upon his knees ;
Save that pale aspect, where the eye, though dim,
Held all the light that shone on earth for him.

XVIII.

The foe arrives, who long had search'd the field,
Their triumph nought till Lara too should yield ;
They would remove him, but they see 't were vain,
And he regards them with a calm disdain,
That rose to reconcile him with his fate,
And that escape to death from living hate :
And Otho comes, and leaping from his steed,

Looks on the bleeding foe that made him bleed,
And questions of his state; he answers not,
Scarce glances on him as on one forgot,
And turns to Kaled : each remaining word
They understood not, if distinctly heard ;
His dying tones are in that other tongue,
To which some strange remembrance wildly clung.
They spake of other scenes, but what — is known
To Kaled, whom their meaning reach'd alone ;
And he replied, though faintly, to their sound,
While gazed the rest in dumb amazement round ;
They seem'd even then — that twain — unto the last
To half forget the present in the past ;
To share between themselves some separate fate,
Whose darkness none beside should penetrate.

XIX.

Their words, though faint, were many — from the tone
Their import those who heard could judge alone ;
From this, you might have deem'd young Kaled's death
More near than Lara's by his voice and breath,
So sad, so deep, and hesitating broke
The accents his scarce-moving pale lips spoke ;
But Lara's voice, though low, at first was clear
And calm, till murmuring death gasp'd hoarsely near ;

But from his visage little could we guess,
So unrepentant, dark, and passionless.
Save that when struggling nearer to his last,
Upon that page his eye was kindly cast;
And once, as Kaled's answering accents ceased,
Rose Lara's hand, and pointed to the East:
Whether (as then the breaking sun from high
Roll'd back the clouds) the morrow caught his eye,
Or that 't was chance, or some remember'd scene
That raised his arm to point where such had been,
Scarce Kaled seem'd to know, but turn'd away,
As if his heart abhorr'd that coming day,
And shrunk his glance before that morning light
To look on Lara's brow — where all grew night.
Yet sense seem'd left, though better were its loss;
For when one near display'd the absolving cross,
And proffer'd to his touch the holy bead,
Of which his parting soul might own the need,
He look'd upon it with an eye profane,
And smiled — Heaven pardon! if 't were with disdain:
And Kaled, though he spoke not, nor withdrew
From Lara's face his fix'd despairing view,
With brow repulsive, and with gesture swift,
Flung back the hand which held the sacred gift,
As if such but disturb'd the expiring man,
Nor seem'd to know his life but *then* began,
That life of Immortality, secure,
To none, save them whose faith in Christ is sure.

XX.

But gasping heaved the breath that Lara drew,
And dull the film along his dim eye grew:
His limbs stretch'd fluttering, and his head droop'd o'er
The weak yet still untiring knee that bore;
He press'd the hand he held upon his heart —
It beats no more, but Kaled will not part
With the cold grasp, but feels, and feels in vain,
For that faint throb which answers not again.
" It beats!" — Away, thou dreamer! he is gone —
It once was Lara which thou look'st upon.

XXI.

He gazed, as if not yet had pass'd away
The haughty spirit of that humble clay;
And those around have roused him from his trance,
But cannot tear from thence his fixed glance;
And when, in raising him from where he bore
Within his arms the form that felt no more,
He saw the head his breast would still sustain
Roll down like earth to earth upon the plain,
He did not dash himself thereby, nor tear
The glossy tendrils of his raven hair,
But strove to stand and gaze, but reel'd and fell,
Scarce breathing more than that he loved so well.
Than that *he* loved! Oh! never yet beneath
The breast of man such trusty love may breathe!

That trying moment hath at once reveal'd
The secret long and yet but half conceal'd:
In baring to revive that lifeless breast,
Its grief seem'd ended, but the sex confess'd:
And life return'd, and Kaled felt no shame —
What now to her was Womanhood or Fame?

XXII.

And Lara sleeps not where his fathers sleep,
But where he died his grave was dug as deep;
Nor is his mortal slumber less profound,
Though priest nor bless'd, nor marble deck'd the
    mound;
And he was mourn'd by one whose quiet grief,
Less loud, outlasts a people's for their chief.
Vain was all question ask'd her of the past,
And vain e'en menace — silent to the last;
She told nor whence nor why she left behind
Her all for one who seem'd but little kind.
Why did she love him? Curious fool !— be still —
Is human love the growth of human will?
To her he might be gentleness: the stern
Have deeper thoughts than your dull eyes discern;
And when they love, your smilers guess not how
Beats the strong heart though less the lips avow.
They were not common links that form'd the chain
That bound to Lara Kaled's heart and brain;
But that wild tale she brook'd not to unfold,
And seal'd is now each lip that could have told.

XXIII.

They laid him in the earth, and on his breast,
Besides the wound that sent his soul to rest,
They found the scatter'd dints of many a scar,
Which were not planted there in recent war;
Where'er had pass'd his summer years of life,
It seems they vanish'd in a land of strife;
But all unknown his glory or his guilt,
These only told that somewhere blood was spilt;
And Ezzelin, who might have spoken the past,
Return'd no more — that night appear'd his last.

XXIV.

Upon that night (a peasant's is the tale)
A Serf that cross'd the intervening vale,
When Cynthia's light almost gave way to morn,
And nearly veil'd in mist her waning horn;
A Serf, that rose betimes to thread the wood,
And hew the bough that bought his children's food,
Pass'd by the river that divides the plain
Of Otho's lands and Lara's broad domain:
He heard a tramp — a horse and horseman broke
From out the wood — before him was a cloak
Wrapped round some burthen at his saddle-bow,
Bent was his head, and hidden was his brow.
Roused by the sudden sight at such a time,
And some foreboding that it might be crime,

Himself unheeded watch'd the stranger's course,
Who reach'd the river, bounded from his horse,
And lifting thence the burthen which he bore,
Heaved up the bank and dash'd it from the shore,
Then paused, and look'd, and turn'd and seem'd to
    watch,
And still another hurried glance would snatch,
And follow with his step the stream that flow'd,
As if even yet too much its surface show'd.
At once he started, stoop'd, around him strown
The winter floods had scatter'd heaps of stone:
Of these the heaviest thence he gather'd there,
And slung them with a more than common care.
Meantime the Serf had crept to where, unseen,
Himself might safely mark what this might mean:
He caught a glimpse, as of a floating breast,
And something glitter'd starlike on the vest;
But ere he well could mark the buoyant trunk,
A massy fragment smote it, and it sunk:
It rose again, but indistinct to view,
And left the waters of a purple hue,
Then deeply disappear'd: the horseman gazed
Till ebb'd the latest eddy it had raised;
Then, turning, vaulted on his pawing steed,
And instant spurr'd him into panting speed.
His face was mask'd — the features of the dead,
If dead it were, escaped the observer's dread;
But if, in sooth, a star its bosom bore,
Such is the badge that knighthood ever wore,

And such 't is known Sir Ezzelin had worn
Upon the night that led to such a morn.
If thus he perish'd, Heaven receive his soul!
His undiscover'd limbs to ocean roll;
And charity upon the hope would dwell,
It was not Lara's hand by which he fell.

XXV.

And Kaled — Lara — Ezzelin, are gone,
Alike without their monumental stone!
The first, all efforts vainly strove to wean
From lingering where her chieftain's blood had
    been:
Grief had so tamed a spirit once too proud,
Her tears were few, her wailing never loud.
But furious would you tear her from the spot
Where yet she scarce believed that he was not,
Her eye shot forth with all the living fire
That haunts the tigress in her whelpless ire;
But left to waste her weary moments there,
She talked all idly unto shapes of air,
Such as the busy brain of Sorrow paints,
And woos to listen to her fond complaints;
And she would sit beneath the very tree,
Where lay his drooping head upon her knee;
And in that posture where she saw him fall,
His words, his looks, his dying grasp recall;
And she had shorn, but saved her raven hair,
And oft would snatch it from her bosom there,

And fold and press it gently to the ground,
As if she stanch'd anew some phantom's wound.
Herself would question, and for him reply;
Then rising, start, and beckon him to fly
From some imagined spectre in pursuit;
Then seat her down upon some linden's root,
And hide her visage with her meagre hand,
Or trace strange characters along the sand.
This could not last — she lies by him she loved;
Her tale untold — her truth too dearly proved.

www.ingramcontent.com/pod-product-compliance
Lightning Source LLC
Chambersburg PA
CBHW031450160426
43195CB00010BB/923